Teaching Tessellating Art

Activities and Transparency Masters

Jill Britton
Walter Britton

Dale Seymour Publications

Dedicated to Dale Seymour and George Escher in appreciation for their invaluable encouragement.

Grateful acknowledgement is made to Cordon Art in Baarn, Holland, exclusive worldwide representatives of the M. C. Escher heirs, for permission to reproduce the following designs of M. C. Escher.

p. 62, Symmetry Drawing E 105

p. 97, Symmetry Drawing E 75

p. 106, Symmetry Drawing E 104

p. 121, Reptiles

p. 125, Symmetry Drawing E 25

p. 137, Symmetry Drawing E 44

p. 155, Symmetry Drawing E 35

p. 161, Metamorphosis I

p. 167, Symmetry Drawing E 117

p. 177, Symmetry Drawing E 97

p. 187, Symmetry Drawing E 63

p. 193, Symmetry Drawing E 96

p. 200, Symmetry Drawing E 67

cover art (center), Symmetry Drawing E 96

Acknowledgement is made to the following artists for use of their original tessellations.

pp. 66, 67, 69, 70, 71, 94, 104, 118, 119, 134, 135, 150, 151, 174, 205 Steve Dawson

pp. 90, 95 Henry Furmanowicz

pp. 84, 88 Lyda Kobylansky

p. 254 Paul Lariviere

p. 214 Shiela Le Blanc

p. 147 ("Tisha") Stephen Makris

p. 255 Tanya L. McLain

p. 92 Nick Zannella

Managing Editor: Michael Kane
Project Editor: Mali Apple
Production: Karen Edmonds
Design: John F. Kelly
Cover Design: David Woods

Order number DS21126
ISBN 0-86651-596-8

4 5 6 7 8 9 10 11-MA-96 95 94

DALE
SEYMOUR
PUBLICATIONS
P.O. BOX 10888
PALO ALTO, CA 94303

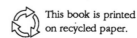

This book is printed on recycled paper.

Contents

Introduction

This companion book to *Introduction to Tessellations* contains transparency masters, duplication masters, and innovative activities for teaching tessellating art.

In Part One you will learn how to make professional-quality transparencies from the paper masters in this book—including advise on how to select the appropriate machine process and transparency film, how to mount transparencies with hinged overlays on frames, and how to incorporate color. A few physical considerations that will help promote the effective use of the transparencies in an instructional setting will also be examined.

In Part Two you will find the transparency masters—the same masters that were used by the author to make the transparencies for her presentation "Geometry and the Art of M. C. Escher." Some masters are preceded by processing and assembling instructions. You will also find detailed instructions about when and how to use each of the transparencies, and an accompanying commentary that you may quote directly or paraphrase. Suggestions for simple student activities to either precede or accompany the transparencies have been included where appropriate—with duplication masters, where required.

The transparency masters follow in sequence selected pages of chapter 4 and all of chapter 7 of *Introduction to Tessellations*. Transparency masters on simple polygonal tessellations are included so you may equip your students with sufficient background knowledge on tessellations to be able to study in depth the material in chapters 4 and 7.

In Part Three you will find suggestions for workshop activities, including explorations with graph paper, making a tessellating template, drawing a tessellation with a template, turning the template into a pop-up sponge jigsaw puzzle, and printing a tessellation with either a sponge or a homemade rubber stamp. You will even find directions for printing your own tessellating T-shirt!

In Part Four you will explore the use of a microcomputer to produce tessellations. A brief analysis of computer programs and simple steps for creating tessellating art with a typical paint or draw program are included.

Part One

Making the Transparencies

In a few seconds, anyone can turn the image on a paper master in this book into a transparent image on a sheet of transparent film. The result, a transparency, can then be placed on the stage of an overhead projector and the image projected onto a viewing screen. All that is required is the proper equipment and materials.

Once you have selected the master, the image must be transferred to transparency film. Over the years, many processes have been developed to accomplish this. The two most frequently used—the *photocopy method* and the *thermal method*—will be considered here.

The Photocopy Method

If you have access to a photocopier, you can make transparencies. Manufacturers of transparency films make film for virtually every photocopier on the market. Different copiers require different film. The supplier of your copy equipment or a supplier of transparency films should be able to help you select the proper film.

Most transparency film for photocopiers comes in 8½-by-11-inch sheets and is designed to project a

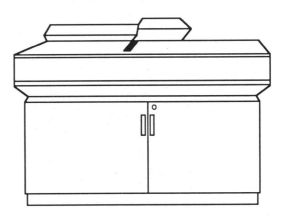

Figure 1

black image on a clear background. With tinted film, it will project a black image on a single color background, including yellow, green, blue, and red. Some photocopiers feature cartridges that will produce a single color image on a clear background or on a single color background of a contrasting color.

Making a transparency by the photocopy method is essentially the same as making a photocopy. The visual information is printed on the transparency film rather than on paper. You can copy directly from the pages of bound volumes, such as this book, as well as from single sheets.

In many schools, teachers will not have direct access to a photocopier and must employ the services of a technician. Most technicians will not take the time to center the visual information. In these circumstances, photocopy transparencies can be mounted in "cut-to-size" frames for a more professional-looking product (see "Frames").

The photocopy method is quick and produces high-quality, finely detailed transparencies. However. you will find that the image printed on the film is translucent. We prefer the density of the image that is burned into the film in the thermal method and tend to use the photocopy method only for gray-toned masters.

Once you start teaching tessellating art, you will start compiling your own portfolio of original student artwork. Transparencies of these works can be added to the student work in this book for a more personal touch. The enlargement and reduction capabilities of most photocopiers will allow you to produce images of appropriate size on the transparency film.

Incidentally, colored artwork can be turned into colored transparencies at printing centers that have a color copier. Unfortunately, the cost per transparency ranges from 10 to 30 times the cost of a *black-on-clear* photocopy transparency.

The Thermal Method

With equal ease and greater convenience, transparencies can also be prepared using thermal transparency makers (see Figure 2). These same machines have been used for years by teachers to prepare alcohol duplicating masters.

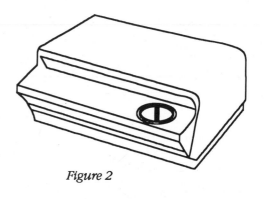

The visual information must be on a sheet of paper that will pass through the machine; it is not possible to copy directly from a book. All markings on the master must contain carbon, such as found in soft lead pencil, printing ink, and photocopy toner. These markings absorb heat, and the resulting increase in temperature affects the film, forming an image on it in a few seconds. The slower the setting on the machine, the longer the heat transfer and the greater the effect on the film. Blemishes on the conveyer belt of the transparency maker can also affect the film. Liquid belt cleaner will remove small specs of carbon but major blemishes may call for replacement of the belt.

Figure 2

We recommend that you process photocopies of the transparency masters in this book rather than the masters themselves. This will eliminate the possibility of damage to the masters due to inappropriate processing, say, using too slow a setting. (Carbon will bond to the film at too slow a setting, and portions of the image could be stripped from the master when you remove the film.) With quality copiers, using a photocopy also guarantees an even distribution of carbon on the master. Unexpected specs of carbon on the master photocopy can be scraped off easily with a stylus or razor blade (single-edged for safety). Remember, only the carbon affects the film!

Manufacturers produce a variety of transparency films for use with thermal transparency makers. The resulting image varies in quality from film to film and from manufacturer to manufacturer. With some films—those without a chemical donor sheet—the film is in direct contact with the master photocopy during processing. The procedure is simple: a sheet of film is positioned on top of the master photocopy (with the notch on the film in the upper right hand corner) and the assembly is passed face up through the thermal transparency maker. For films with a donor sheet, the donor sheet must be positioned between the film and the master photocopy. With practice, you will learn the appropriate setting to use on the exposure dial of the transparency maker for each type of film—the slower the speed, the longer the exposure.

We have tested *black-on-clear* (black image on a clear background) thermal films supplied to us by several manufacturers of transparency films (see the list at the end of Part One) and recommend the type without a donor sheet. These films come in a variety of weights: light (2 mil thick), medium (4 mil thick), and heavy (7 mil thick). We recommend a light weight film for general usage and a medium weight when extra thickness is required. Unfortunately, black-on-clear thermal films with a donor sheet tend to yellow with age. We have transparencies made with a film without a donor sheet that are over twenty years old and whose images are as sharp and whose backgrounds are as clear as the day they were processed.

For *black-on-colored* (black image on a yellow, green, blue, or red background) thermal transparency films, we also recommend only the type without a donor sheet. A light weight film is adequate for general use.

Manufacturers also produce *colored-on-clear* (green, blue, red, or purple image on a clear background) thermal films. All those tested produced satisfactory results. The type without a donor sheet require an extremely slow speed for complete exposure of the film with masters like Escher's "Lizard I," "Lizard II," "Dogs," and "Study of Regular Division of the Plane with Human Figures." Those films with a donor sheet produce comparable results—in more intense colors and at a lower cost. They require a moderate processing speed, a little slower than that used with black-on-clear or black-on-colored films.

In what follows, we will also suggest selective use of high impact *reverse-image* (brilliant yellow image on a blue, green, red, or violet background) thermal films. Several of the manufacturers produce an acceptable version of such a film.

All thermal transparencies are both heat and light sensitive. They should be stored in a dark place and separated by pieces of paper to prevent scratching.

Frames

A *frame* is a sturdy cardboard or plastic structure to which a sheet of transparency film can be attached. The frame blocks light around the edge of the film, adds rigidity for ease of handling and storage, and provides a margin for brief notes and identification.

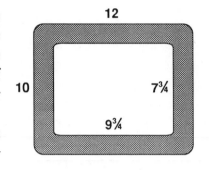

Figure 3

The frame should be about 10-by-12 inches overall. The opening should be approximately 7¾-by-9¾ inches (see Figure 3). Frames that meet these specifications are available from most manufacturers of transparency films and suppliers of audiovisual materials.

In this book, only transparencies that involve an overlay or overlays were designed to be mounted in a frame. For those transparencies that consist of a single sheet of film, we have made full use of the available surface of the film as required. For ease of handling, you may wish to use a medium weight thermal film for unmounted transparencies.

Overlays

In what follows, we will consider the procedure for mounting transparencies that include hinged overlays on frames. While transparencies consisting of a single sheet of transparency film are extremely useful, it is the overlay technique that has sold many teachers on overhead projection.

The technique involves superimposing one or more single sheets of transparency film, called *overlays*, over a fixed sheet of film, referred to as the *base*. The sequence of the overlays makes it possible to discuss each phase of a concept as it relates to the whole. Overlays can be added one at a time to develop a complicated concept in stages, or they can be removed one by one to simplify a complicated concept by reducing it to its simplest components.

Hinged Overlay

The most common type of transparency consists of a base with a single hinged overlay. The base is taped to the *back* of a frame, face down (see Figure 4). (Tape the sides and then the corners.) The overlay is hinged to the *front* of the frame, face up, so it can be flipped into place on top of the base when needed. As hinges, use 2-inch tape strips or purchase virtually indestructible self-adhesive silvered Mylar hinges (available from AVCOM®).

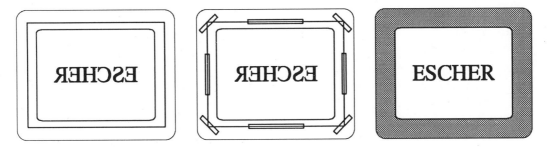

Figure 4

Although any edge of the overlay can be hinged, we recommend that you use either the left-hand or right-hand edge. If you are right-handed, you will find that locating your hinges on the left-hand edge will allow you to flip the overlay into place with your left hand while pointing to visual information of interest with your right hand (see Figure 5).

Registration marks in the corners of transparencies with overlay(s) will facilitate alignment.

Several of the transparencies in this book were designed to include more than one hinged overlay. In some of the transparencies, the overlays are intended to be hinged on the same edge, overlay 2 to be positioned on top of overlay 1, hinge on top of hinge. Once the first overlay is in place, the second is flipped into place on top of it (see Figure 6).

In other transparencies, one of the overlays is intended to be hinged along its left-hand edge (*LH overlay*) and the other along its right-hand edge (*RH overlay*). The overlays can be used independently (that is, the first can be removed before the second is flipped into place), or they can be superimposed one on top of the other for a cumulative effect (see Figure 7).

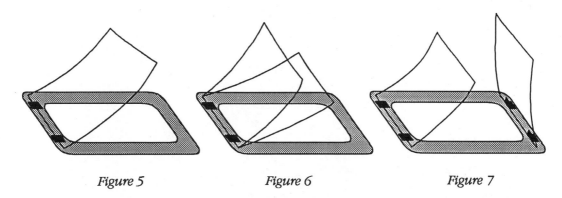

Figure 5   *Figure 6*   *Figure 7*

A few transparencies have a combination of these two strategies. As the layers of film accumulate, the intensity of the projected image diminishes. We recommend you select a light weight thermal film for general usage. Note that the transparencies have been designed so that no more than two overlays are in place at any one time.

Unless indicated otherwise, the transparencies have also been designed to be shown in a *vertical format*—that is, with the longer edges of the film oriented vertically and with any hinges added along the longer sides of the frame. In a *horizontal format,* the longer edges are oriented horizontally and any hinges are added along the shorter sides of the frame.

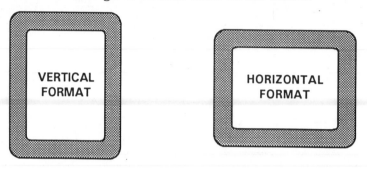

Figure 8. Vertical format (left) and horizontal format (right).

Once an overlay is properly aligned, secure its top and bottom edges with tape to maintain its position as the hinges are attached. Remove the restraining tape once the hinges are in place.

If you are using the thermal method, the registration marks on the master photocopy of the base of transparencies with overlay(s) will help you position the film so that the visual information will be centered (see Figure 9). Corresponding LH overlays and RH overlays should be processed off center relative to the base to avoid the accidental catching of the right-hand edge of a LH overlay in any right-hand hinges, and vice versa.

Thus a LH overlay is processed off center to allow for additional acetate on its left-hand edge, and a RH overlay to allow for additional acetate on its right-hand edge. This is accomplished by shifting the transparency film approximately one-eighth of an inch to the left or right, respectively, of the position in which it would have been placed if it were centered. The registration marks will assist you in this endeavor (see Figure 10).

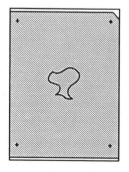

Figure 9. Base.   *Figure 10. LH overlay (left) and RH overlay (right).*

If the overlays are hinged on the same side, the upper overlay (that is, overlay 2) should be processed still further off center for easier handling. This is accomplished by shifting the film an additional one-eighth of an inch to the left or right for LH overlays and RH overlays respectively. If you are using a photocopy method you may wish to trim the appropriate edges of the overlays.

Overlays can be subtractive as well as additive. That is, one can start with a complete figure and remove overlays to reach a fundamental result. The methods for hinging are the same, but the use is reversed.

Sliding Overlay

There are occasions when it is desirable to keep an overlay loose to allow complete freedom of movement. Here we have the principle of the *sliding* or *moveable* overlay.

A *sliding overlay* may be a full sheet of transparency film or a small piece of overlay, generally a rectangular piece of film slightly larger than the area to be projected.

Transparencies whose processing instructions include directions to process a piece or pieces of overlay were designed to be used with a corresponding piece or pieces of overlay. Masters are found in the four pages of masters for pieces of overlay at the end of Part Two. We recommend that these pages be processed as *pages* of heavier weight black-on-clear transparency film and then cut into rectangular pieces (see Figure 11).

Trim each rectangle to within one-eighth inch of the serrated dividing line. Do not further reduce the size of the transparent rectangle—or cut out the region on it—unless instructed to do so.

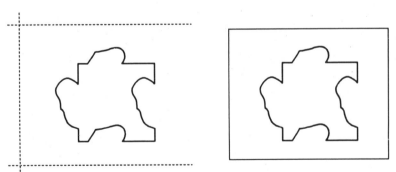

Figure 11

Adding Color

Color can be used in a transparency to show relationships, to distinguish regions, and to add interest and eye appeal. Color must be transparent and can be added in a variety of ways.

The simplest way to add color is to add an overlay of colored-on-clear transparency film (see "Machine Processes").

An effective way to add colored points or lines is to use color projection pens. Both water-soluble and permanent inks project beautifully. Water-soluble inks can be removed with water but tend to rub off with use. Permanent colors must be removed with alcohol. (A *dilute* alcohol solution is recommended to avoid visible damage to the chemical coating on the transparency film.)

You can use a projection pen with a shading stroke to color small areas but we do not recommend that shading be used to fill in large areas (such as modified polygons). Overlapping strokes build up layers of color and are visually distracting. A compromise is to create a striped effect with parallel lines drawn from boundary to boundary of the region to be colored (see Figure 12).

Figure 12

The usual method of adding large blocks of color is to use sheets of color-projecting self-adhesive film, available in a variety of colors. Red, blue, and green are recommended for general work. Most manufacturers of transparency films produce their own line of adhesive films.

To use the adhesive film, cut a piece (with its paper backing) slightly larger than needed. Remove the paper backing and apply the adhesive side of the film directly to the front or back of the transparency over the region to be colored. If wrinkles occur, smooth them out. The piece can be removed and reapplied. Then cut around the boundary of the region with a stylus or razor blade, being careful to cut through only the adhesive film and not the transparency film underneath (see Figure 13). Peel off the excess adhesive film. The effect is well worth the effort.

Figure 13

Using Transparencies Effectively

Once you have processed, mounted, and colored your transparencies, you will be ready to use them in an instructional setting. A few physical considerations should be taken into account to ensure that the transparencies are used effectively.

The overhead projector should be as accessible as a blackboard and located so that any projected image is large enough to fill the viewing screen.

In most rooms, the height of the screen will require that the head of the projector be tilted slightly. Unfortunately, the top of the image will then project wider than the bottom, a distortion known as the *keystone effect* (see Figure 14). Although evident when any projection device is used, the effect is very pronounced in overhead projection because the projector is placed so close to the screen.

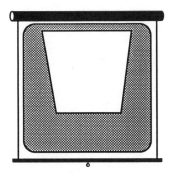

Figure 14. The keystone effect.

Owing to the geometric content of the transparencies in this book, the keystone effect will prove very deceptive and undesirable. To reduce the distortion, it is a good idea to tilt the top of the screen a bit forward (see Figure 15). A good rule of thumb is to have an angle of about 90° between the screen and the center of the projection head. Tiltable screens that can minimize the keystone effect are available commercially.

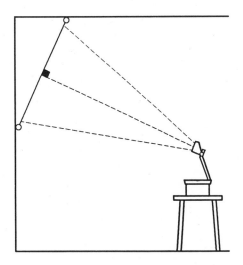

Figure 15

The stage of an overhead projector is quite literally that—a projection stage. Remember to point at the transparency, rather than at the screen, when you draw attention to visual information of interest.

Manufacturers of Transparency Materials

Arkwright Inc., 538 Main Street, Fiskeville, Rhode Island 02823-0139

AVCOM® Systems, Inc., P.O. Box 977, 250 Cox Lane, Cutchogue, New York 11935

Folex® Film Systems, 21 S. Limerick Road, Royesford, Pennsylvania 19468

Labelon® Corp., 10 Chapin Street, Canandaigua, New York 14424-1589

Letraset™, 40 Eisenhower Drive, Paramus, New Jersey 07653

3M Company, Visual Systems Division, 3M Austin Center, Building A145-5N-01, Austin, Texas 78769-2963

Part Two

The Transparency Masters

The preparation of professional quality transparencies from the masters in Part Two presumes a familiarity with the material presented in Part One. We reiterate the following:

- Where appropriate, the master or masters for each of the transparencies is preceded by processing and assembly instructions. You will also find comments as to both when and how to use the transparency and an accompanying commentary (in *italics*) that you may quote directly or paraphrase.

- Unless otherwise indicated, the use of a thermal method with light weight (2 mil) black-on-clear transparency film is recommended.

- Process photocopies of the transparency masters rather than the masters themselves.

- Only transparencies that include hinged overlays were designed to be mounted in frames. For transparencies that consist of a single sheet of film, you may wish to use a medium weight (4 mil) transparency film.

- Unless otherwise indicated, the transparencies have been designed to be shown in a vertical format.

- The master or masters for each transparency have been suitably labelled. Where significant, the location of the hinges for transparencies that include hinged overlays has been specified.

- Registration marks have been placed in the corners of transparencies that include hinged overlays to facilitate alignment.

- Transparencies whose processing instructions include direction to process a piece or pieces of overlay were designed to be used with a corresponding piece or pieces of overlay. Masters are found in the four pages of masters for pieces of overlay at the end of Part Two. We recommend that these pages be processed as pages of heavier weight black-on-clear transparency film and then cut into rectangular pieces, each trimmed to within one-eighth of an inch of the serrated dividing line. Do not further reduce the size of the transparent rectangle—or cut out the region on it—unless instructed to do so.

- Recommendations have been made as to which regions to highlight with color, preferably with color-projecting adhesive film. Practice applying and trimming the adhesive film before proceeding.

Transformations of the Plane

Assembly Instructions

Process the piece of overlay.

Commentary

Understanding symmetry is essential to understanding of Escher art—and understanding symmetry involves a familiarity with the movements that mathematicians call transformations.

Show the transparency.

A transformation may be thought of as a motion that moves a figure from one location on a plane to a new location on that plane.

Place the arrow on the piece of overlay to coincide with the large arrow at the left of the section titled Translation. Slide the piece of overlay down and to the right, in the direction of the smaller arrow, until the arrow on the overlay coincides with the arrow at the right of that section.

If we move a figure to a new location by sliding it a fixed distance in a fixed direction, the motion is the transformation we call a translation *or a* slide.

Repeat the process, using the large arrow at the left of the section titled Rotation. Press the tip of a sharp pencil to the marked point to anchor the piece of overlay to the transparency. Then turn the piece of overlay through an appropriate angle about that point, in the direction of the smaller arrow, until the arrow on the overlay coincides with the arrow at the right of that section.

If we move a figure to a new location by turning it through a fixed angle about a fixed point, the motion is referred to as a rotation *or* turn. *The point about which the figure is rotated is called the* center of rotation. *The angle through which the figure turns is called the* angle of rotation.

Repeat the process again, using the arrow at the left of the section titled Reflection. Lift the piece of overlay, then flip it over and to the right, "about" the marked line. The arrow on the overlay should coincide with the arrow at the right of that section.

> *If we move a figure to a new location by flipping it about a fixed line, the motion is called a* reflection *or flip. It is called a reflection because, if a mirror were placed along the line, the transformed figure would coincide with the mirror image of the figure in its original location. The fixed line about which the figure is flipped is called the* line of reflection.

Repeat the process one last time, using the arrow at the left of the section titled Glide Reflection. Lift the piece of overlay, then flip it over and to the right, "about" the marked line. Slide it downward in a direction parallel to that line until the arrow on the overlay coincides with the arrow at the right of that section.

> *In the final type of transformation, we combine the motions of reflection and translation to move a figure to its new location—first by flipping it about a fixed line, then by sliding it a fixed distance in a direction parallel to that line. This motion is called a* glide-reflection. *We could, of course, have performed the steps in reverse order, sliding the figure first and then reflecting it. The result would be the same.*

You might provide each student with a paper copy of the transparency master and a transparent copy of the piece of overlay for individual study. If possible, you should also provide each student with a mirror to study reflection.

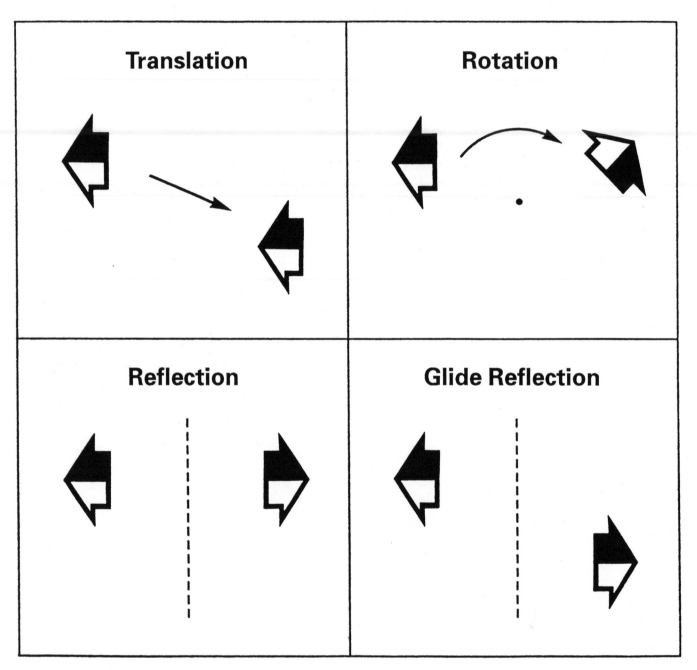

Translation

Rotation

Reflection

Glide Reflection

Transparency 1

Reflective Symmetry

Assembly Instructions

Process the piece of overlay.

Commentary

The most effective way to use this visual is to provide each student with a paper copy of the clown face.

Show the transparency base.

Most of us would view the face of this clown as being symmetric—but what do we mean by the word symmetric?

Add the overlay.

The features on one side of the clown face have matching features on the other side. If you were to fold the figure along this vertical line, one half would coincide with the other half.

Ask the students to add the vertical line to their paper copies, then to fold them along that line.

Place the figure on the piece of overlay to coincide with the left half of the clown face on the transparency base. Flip the piece of overlay about the vertical line.

If we flip the clown face about the vertical line, the left side coincides exactly with the right side. If you were to place a mirror along this line, you would find that the mirror image of one half of the clown face is exactly the same as the other half. The two halves are mirror images of each other.

If students can be provided with mirrors, let them verify this fact for themselves.

We say that the figure has reflective symmetry, *and the vertical line is its* line *of* reflection. *This type of symmetry is what the word* symmetry *means to most people.*

Transparency 2

Overlay

Rotational Symmetry

Assembly Instructions

Make two copies of the transparency.

Commentary

Show one copy of the transparency.

> *This figure has a different kind of symmetry.*

Rotate the transparency 120°.

> *It is possible to rotate the figure through less than one full turn so its appearance does not change. It is said to have* rotational symmetry. *The point about which the figure turns is called the* center of rotation.

Superimpose the second copy of the transparency on the first. Press the tip of a sharp pencil to the center of rotation (center point) to anchor the two layers. Rotate the upper layer through successive increments of 120° until it returns to its starting position.

> *If we superimpose the figure on itself, the two figures will coincide exactly three times in one full turn. We say that the figure has* three-fold (3-fold) *rotational symmetry. What is the size of the angle between successive fits? (120°) We call this the* angle of rotation.

> *A figure with 2-fold rotational symmetry would coincide exactly twice in one full turn. What is the size of the angle between successive fits if a figure has 2-fold symmetry? (180°)*

> *How would you find the size of the angle between successive fits if a figure has 4-fold symmetry? (360°/4 = 90°)*

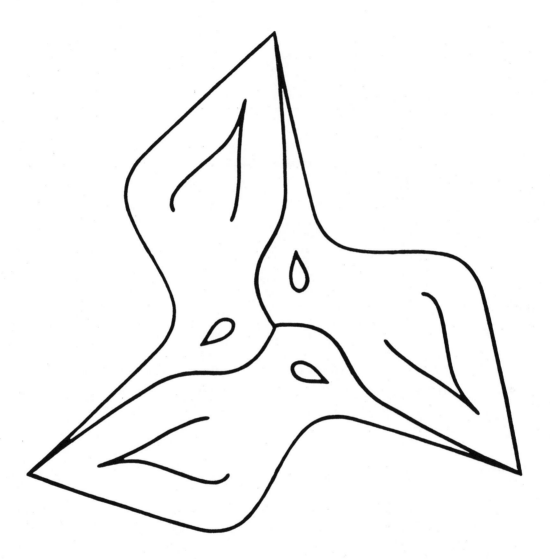

Transparency 3

Translational Symmetry and Glide-Reflection Symmetry

Assembly Instructions

Process the piece of overlay. You could use colored-on-clear film for LH overlay 1.

Commentary

Show the transparency base.

> *The trail left on a sandy beach by a biped hopping on one foot has yet another kind of symmetry.*

Place the figure on the piece of overlay to coincide with the figure on the transparency base. Slide the piece of overlay upwards until the figures again coincide.

> *If the trail were to extend infinitely upwards and downward, then it could be made to coincide with itself by sliding it upwards or downward. The figure is said to have* translational symmetry.

Remove the piece of overlay. Add LH overlay 1 and LH overlay 2.

> *If this biped hops on both feet at the same time, the trail will have both translational and reflective symmetry. The vertical line is the line of reflection.*

Remove LH overlay 2. Add the RH overlay.

> *If this biped walks on both feet the way a human walks, the trail will again have translational symmetry, but it will lack reflective symmetry. It has, instead, a fourth kind of symmetry. If the trail were to extend infinitely upwards and downward, then it could be made to coincide with itself by flipping it about the vertical line and sliding it upwards or downward. (The sequence of transformations can be reversed.) The figure is said to have*

glide-reflection symmetry.

Remove the RH overlay. Return LH overlay 2.

> *Any figure with both translational and reflective symmetry also has, as a natural consequence, glide-reflection symmetry.*

Remove LH overlay 2. Return the RH overlay.

> *This figure has translational and glide-reflection symmetry, but it lacks reflective symmetry.*

Base

Transparency 4

LH Overlay 1

Transparency 4

RH Overlay

Regular Polygons

Commentary

Show the transparency.

> *A regular polygon is a closed geometrical figure with all sides of the same length and all angles of the same measure. Observe that as the number of sides in a regular polygon increases, the closer it comes to appearing like a circle.*

If time permits, explore the names of the polygons shown. They are the equilateral triangle, square, regular pentagon, regular hexagon, regular heptagon, regular octagon, regular nonagon, and regular decagon.

> *Suppose that you are presented with the task of tiling your bathroom floor. Further suppose that you can use only one kind and one size of polygonal tile, and that those tiles must meet side to side and vertex to vertex—without any gaps or overlaps. Which regular polygons could you select to accomplish the task?*

Provide the students with pattern blocks of regular polygons and allow them to experiment. As an alternative to pattern blocks, print the transparency master on cardboard, then have the students cut out several copies of each polygon. Some students may recognize the futility of cutting out polygons with more sides than a hexagon.

Even lacking hands-on experience with the polygons, few students will fail to name the square. Some may suggest the equilateral triangle. A few brave souls may even name the hexagon. You might mention that bees use the regular hexagon exclusively for the shape of the cells in their honeycomb. A piece of honeycomb could be passed around the class to corroborate this statement. It is also likely that someone will name the regular pentagon. These possibilities will be considered in Transparencies 6 and 7.

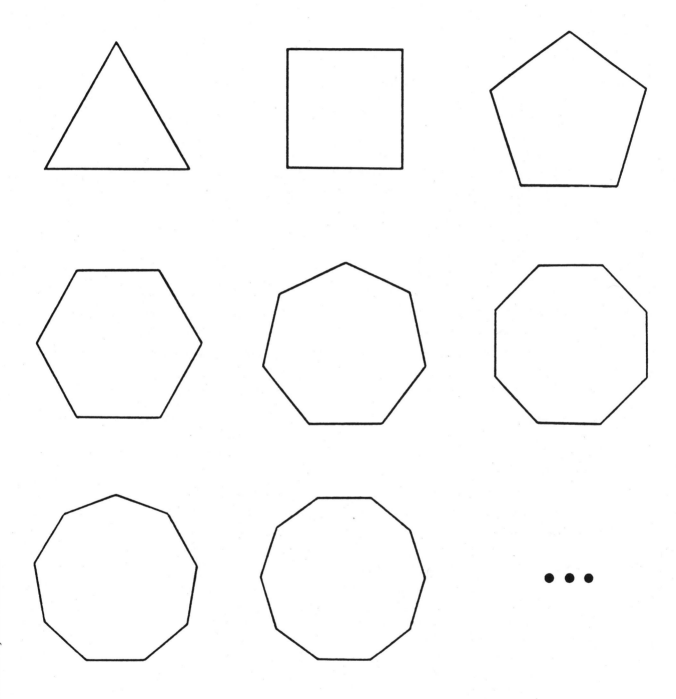

Transparency 5

The Regular Tessellations

Commentary

Show the transparency.

You could tile the floor with equilateral triangles, squares, or regular hexagons. Each of these regular polygons is said to tessellate the plane (from the Latin tessella, which was the small, square stone or tile used in ancient Roman mosaics). Each of the corresponding geometrical designs or patterns is called a tessellation.

In general, a plane tessellation is a pattern of one or more shapes, completely covering the plane without any gaps or overlaps. In the tessellation of equilateral triangles, six triangles meet at every vertex. In the tessellation of squares, four squares meet at every vertex, and in the tessellation of regular hexagons, three hexagons meet at every vertex. We will soon discover the reason for this arrangement.

You may wish to investigate the symmetries of these tessellations, the *regular tessellations*. Make a duplicate of the transparency. Use it like a piece of overlay, sliding, turning, and flipping it as required. You will find that each tessellation has all four kinds of symmetry. Details on the rotational symmetries will be found in *Introduction to Tessellations* (p. 72).

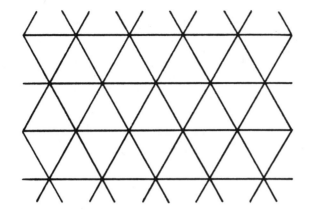

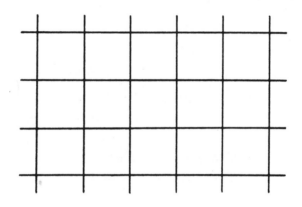

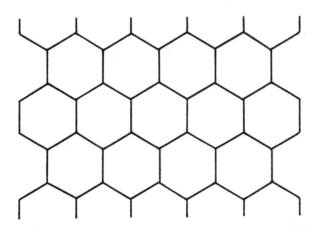

Transparency 6

Tessellating with a Regular Pentagon

Assembly Instructions

Use medium weight black-on-clear film.

Color each pentagon, preferably by covering each with a piece of color-projecting adhesive film; see "Adding Color" in Part One. Carefully cut out the colored pentagons with scissors.

You could also use a copy of the transparency master as a pattern to cut the pentagons out of heavyweight color-projecting plastic. Glue the pattern to the plastic, cut out the pentagons, then tear off the paper pattern from each cutout. Rub off any residual glue.

Commentary

Show the transparency pieces. Then position the pieces so that they share a common vertex and two pairs of sides coincide.

> *If we attempt to tessellate with a regular pentagon, we find that a small gap occurs. A regular pentagon does not tessellate the plane.*

> *A logical question to ask ourselves is: "Why does a gap occur when we try to tessellate the plane with a regular pentagon, but no gaps or overlaps occur when we use an equilateral triangle, a square, or a regular hexagon?"*

> *To answer this question, we will need the measure of the angles of each of the regular polygons.*

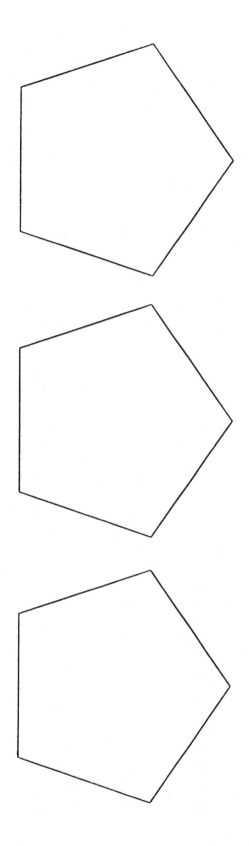

Transparency 7

Angle Measures in Regular Polygons

Assembly Instructions

Color the equilateral triangle, square, and regular hexagon red.

Commentary

Show the transparency.

> *What happens to the size of the angle of a regular polygon as the number of sides of the polygon increases? (It increases—in fact, the measure is approaching 180° as a limit.)*

As you pose the following questions, show Transparency 6 again as required.

> *Why don't we get a gap when we try to tessellate with a square, the most common regular polygon? (The four 90° angles exactly fill the space around a common vertex; 90 divides 360 four times.)*

> *And the equilateral triangle? (The six 60° angles exactly fill the space around a common vertex; 60 divides 360 six times.) And the regular hexagon? (The three 120° angles exactly fill the space around a common vertex; 120 divides 360 three times.)*

> *A regular polygon will tessellate the plane if and only if the measure of its angle in degrees divides 360 exactly. Each angle in a regular pentagon measures 108°. Note that 108 does not divide 360 exactly; regular pentagons cannot tessellate the plane by themselves.*

> *This is the case with the angle measure of a regular 7-, 8-, 9- and 10-sided polygon. Since the size of the angle increases as the number of sides of the polygon increases, the next time we could fill 360° with equal angles would be when we had two angles measuring 180°. It is impossible to have a regular polygon each of whose angles measures 180° (since this is a straight line). We can conclude that, of the regular polygons, only the equilateral triangle, the square, and the regular hexagon tessellate the plane.*

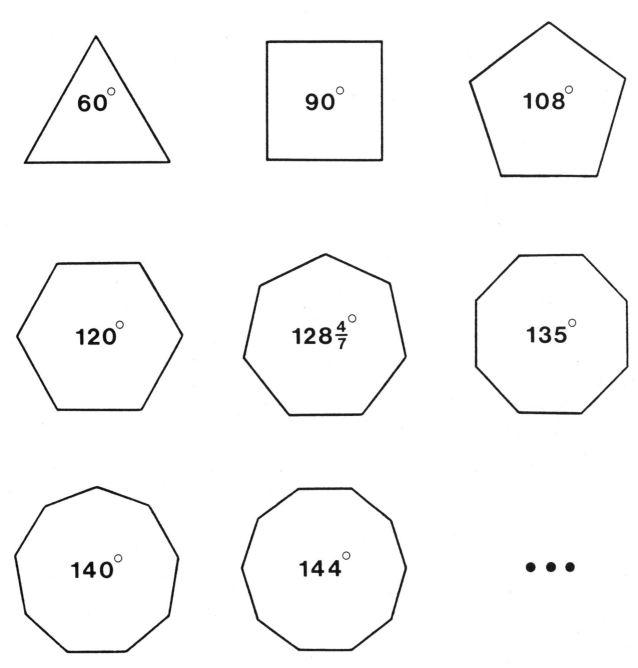

60°

90°

108°

120°

128$\frac{4}{7}$$^{\circ}$

135°

140°

144°

• • •

Transparency 8

Other Polygonal Tessellations

Commentary

Show the transparency.

> *Any rectangle will tessellate the plane—and any parallelogram as well.*

Point to the tessellation in the lower right hand corner.

> *If we are allowed to flip our tiles, not the case with most ceramic ones, parallelograms can be used to make this interesting design.*

You may wish to investigate the symmetries of these tessellations. As before, make a duplicate of the transparency, then use it like a piece of overlay, sliding, turning, and flipping it as required. The tessellation of parallelograms in the lower right-hand corner is particularly interesting. It does not have any vertical lines of reflection. However, if the tessellation is reflected about the vertical line passing through the center of any arbitrary parallelogram and then translated vertically, it will coincide with itself.

> *There are many tessellating irregular polygons. We have considered here only those that will be encountered in what follows.*

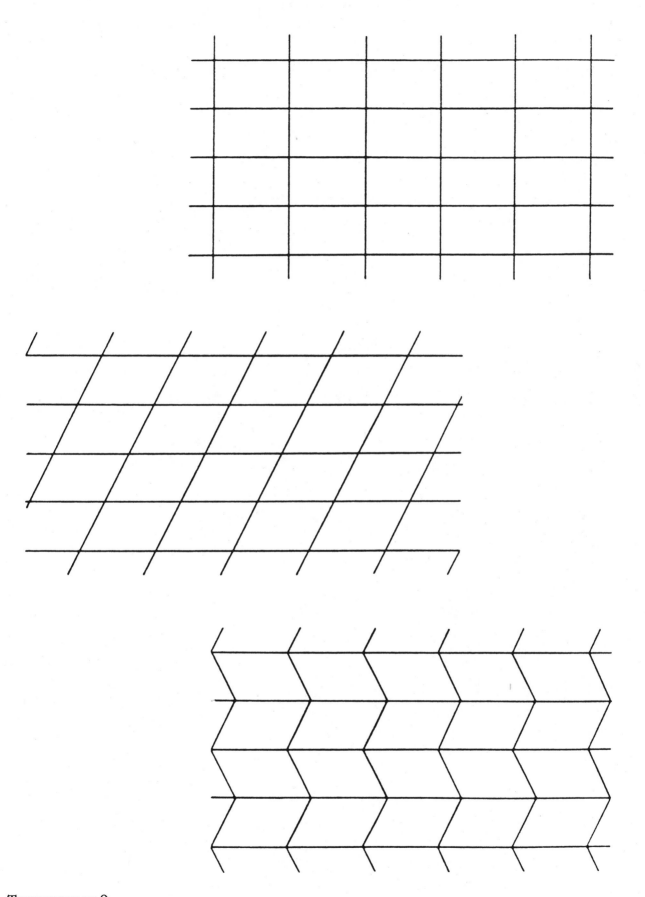

Transparency 9

Scalene Quadrilaterals

Assembly Instructions

Use medium weight black-on-clear film.

Color at least six quadrilaterals, preferably with color-projecting adhesive film, then carefully cut them out. You might also use a copy of the transparency master as a pattern to cut the quadrilaterals out of heavyweight color-projecting plastic.

Commentary

The most effective way to use this visual is to provide each student with a set of quadrilaterals. Print the transparency master on cardboard, then have the students cut out the polygons.

> *Suppose that in your search for the perfect tile, you come across a box of identical scalene quadrilateral tiles.*

Position the transparency pieces on the overhead stage one at a time, taking care to orient them right side up and in such a way that it is apparent that they are identical.

> *The sides of the quadrilateral are of different lengths and its angles are of different sizes and of no specific measure. The immediate reaction is that such a polygon will not tessellate the plane . . . or will it?*

Ask the students to try to tessellate the plane with the quadrilaterals. Caution them to remember that the polygons must meet side to side and vertex to vertex without any gaps or overlaps.

Transparency 10

Tessellating with a Scalene Quadrilateral

Assembly Instructions

Process the pieces of overlay. Color the quadrilateral on piece of overlay 1 (no midpoints) and carefully cut it out. Using the same color, color the quadrilateral on piece of overlay 2 (midpoints).

Commentary

Show the transparency base.

> *Blessed with an incurable optimism, you decide to purchase the box of scalene quadrilateral tiles. Suppose you position a tile on the floor. The angles of the quadrilateral have been labelled for reference.*
>
> *If you wish the tiles to meet side to side and vertex to vertex along the side between the angles labelled b and c, how might you position the next tile? (Most students will suggest that you flip the tile about that side.)*

Place the quadrilateral on piece of overlay 1 to coincide with the quadrilateral on the transparency base. Flip the quadrilateral about the side between angles b and c. Remove the piece of overlay, then add LH overlay 1.

> *Suppose we continue to flip our new quadrilaterals in a circular route about a common vertex.*

Place the quadrilateral on the same piece of overlay to coincide with the quadrilateral on LH overlay 1. Flip the quadrilateral about the side between angles *c* and *d*, then immediately flip it about the side between angles *b* and *c*. Remove the piece of overlay, then add LH overlay 2.

> *Unfortunately, there is a gap. If we study the configuration, we find that the common vertex is surrounded by angles labelled c Since we have no guarantee that the measure of angle c in degrees divides 360 exactly, it is not surprising that the gap*

occurs. Undaunted, you decide to try a new approach.

Remove LH overlays 1 and 2.

> *How else might you position the next tile, if you still wish the tiles to meet side to side and vertex to vertex along the side between angles b and c? (Some student will usually suggest that you turn it.)*

> *To be more specific, we will rotate the quadrilateral 180° about the midpoint of that side.*

Place the quadrilateral on piece of overlay 2 to coincide with the quadrilateral on the transparency base. Press the tip of a sharp pencil to the marked point on the side between angles *b* and *c* to anchor the piece of overlay to the base. Then rotate the piece of overlay 180°. Remove the piece of overlay, then add RH overlay 1.

> *Suppose we continue to rotate our new quadrilaterals 180° about the midpoint of a side in a circular route about a common vertex.*

Place the quadrilateral on the same piece of overlay to coincide with the quadrilateral on RH overlay 1. Rotate the piece of overlay 180° about the marked point on the side between angles *a* and *b*, then immediately rotate it 180° about the marked point on the side between angles *a* and *d*. Remove the piece of overlay, then add RH overlay 2.

> *Eureka! There appears to be no gap. If we study the configuration, we find that the common vertex is surrounded by the four angles of the quadrilateral. It is a well-established theorem in geometry that the sum of the measures of the angles of any quadrilateral is always 360°, or a complete revolution.*

> *Clearly if we take the latter approach, there will never be a gap about any common vertex.*

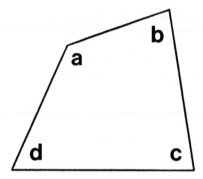

Base

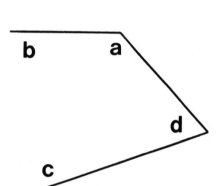

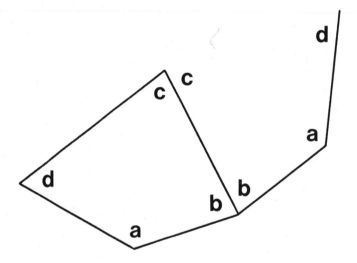

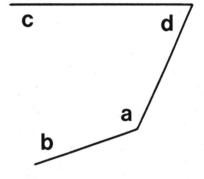

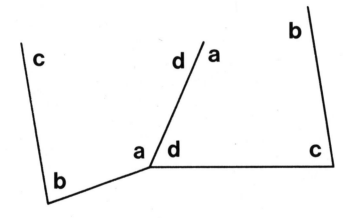

Scalene Quadrilateral and Triangle Tessellations

Commentary

At this point, the question becomes: "Does the pattern continue? Will the scalene quadrilateral tessellate the plane?"

Show Transparency 12.

If we continue to rotate each quadrilateral 180° about the midpoint of each of its sides, we will find that the pattern continues. We can conclude that any quadrilateral will tessellate the plane.

You may wish to investigate the symmetries of this tessellation. As before, make a duplicate of the transparency and use it like a piece of overlay. The tessellation has translational symmetry and 2-fold rotational symmetry about the midpoints of the sides of each quadrilateral.

Show Transparency 13.

Any triangle will also tessellate the plane if we rotate the polygon 180° about the midpoint of each of its sides.

It will take two sets of the triangle's angles to fill 360°. Because the sum of the angles of any triangle is 180°, we find that the tessellation consists of three distinct sets of equidistant parallel lines.

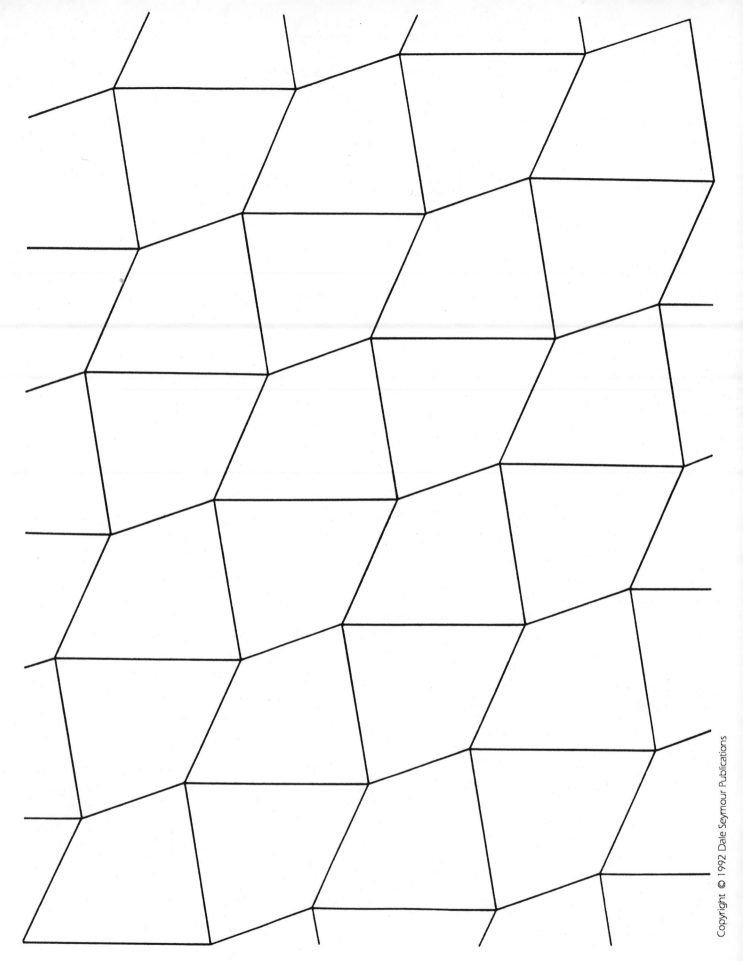

Transparency 12

Transparency 13

Modifying by Translation

Assembly Instructions

Process the pieces of overlay.

Color both modified squares on Transparency 14 with the same color. This will emphasize each figure and the equivalence of the areas of the original and modified figures. To color the *first* modified square: Once Transparency 14 has been assembled, position both LH overlays on top of the transparency base. Cover the modified square *as it appears to the eye* with the adhesive film. Trim the film to conform to the boundary of the modified square. The second modified square on the RH overlay is colored in the usual way.

Color the figure on the base of Transparency 15 and on its piece of overlay with the same color used on Transparency 14.

Commentary

Show the base of Transparency 14.

> *This square will tessellate the plane, as will all squares.*

Add LH overlay 1.

> *Suppose we modify the polygon by adding a protrusion or "bump" to one side. If we wish the modified square to tessellate the plane, the bump must fit into a congruent indentation or "hole."*

> *Suppose we decide to remove the hole from the opposite side.*

Place the modification on the piece of overlay to coincide with the modification on LH overlay 1. Slide the piece of overlay downward until the endpoints of the modification coincide with the lower vertices of the square.

> *We can locate the hole by translating the modification to the opposite side of the square.*

Remove the piece of overlay, then add LH overlay 2.

The modified square has the same area as the original or parent square.

Remove both LH overlays. Add the RH overlay.

We can modify the other set of sides in the same way.

Show the base of Transparency 15.

As before, the modified square has the same area as the parent square.

Place the modified square on the piece of overlay to coincide with the modified square on the transparency base. Slide the piece of overlay upwards until the modified sides again coincide. Repeat the process, sliding downward, to the right, and to the left.

This non-polygonal shape will tessellate the plane. If we translate it upwards, downward, to the left, or to the right, we can see the precise fit. The challenge now is to give some meaning to the shape. Does it suggest anything to you?

Slowly rotate the shape so that the students can see it from different angles. The most effective way to use this visual is to provide each student with a paper copy of the shape so that they can add details that give it a meaning.
    Add the overlay.

The individual who designed this tessellating shape interpreted it as a knight from a chessboard—very appropriate!

Show the base of Transparency 16.

The resulting tessellation is rather dull on its own, but if we add the details that give it a meaning, . . .

Add the overlay.

. . . it is much more interesting.

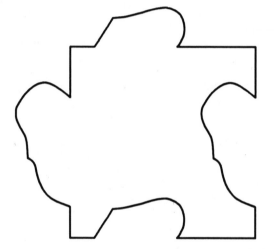

RH Overlay

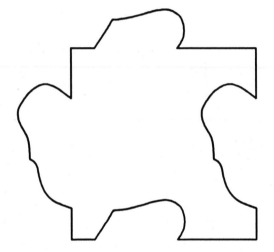

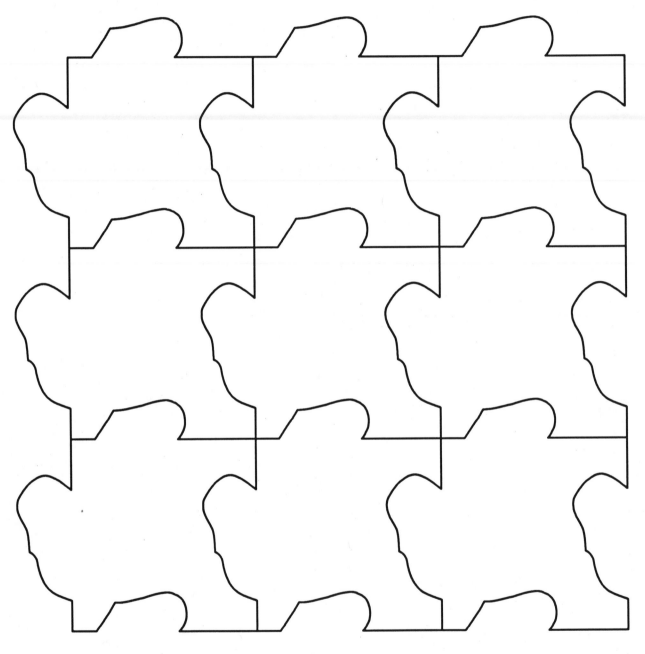

Base

"Pegasus" Tessellating Shape

Assembly Instructions

Color the figure on the transparency base.

Commentary

The master of the creation of tessellating shape was the late Dutch graphic artist M. C. Escher (1898–1972). With extraordinary inventiveness, he created tessellating shapes that resembled birds, fish, lizards, dogs, humans, butterflies, and the occasional creature of his own invention.

Show the transparency with the overlay in place.

A good example of Escher's inventiveness is the non-polygonal shape for his tessellation "Pegasus." Just as in our introductory example, the sides of the parent square have been modified by translation. Note the complexity of the modifications to the two sets of parallel sides.

Remove the overlay.

Without the underlying square in place, it is difficult to immediately identify the polygon that is its basis.

You might make a duplicate of the "Pegasus," color it as on the transparency base, trim it to a manageable size, and use it like a piece of overlay to confirm the precise fits.

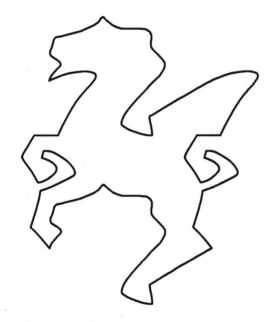

Copyright © 1992 Dale Seymour Publications

Transparency 17

Overlay

"Pegasus"

Assembly Instructions

Make two copies of the transparency base using a photocopy method. To guarantee alignment, use the same photocopy method for the overlay.

Commentary

Show the transparency base.

"Pegasus" is one of Escher's most striking tessellations.

Add the overlay.

It we superimpose the grid of squares that is its basis, we find that each winged horse fits in its parent square in exactly the same way as its fellow horses.

Remove the overlay. Superimpose the second copy of "Pegasus" on the first. Slide it in a variety of directions until a horse coincides with a horse.

*The tessellation has **only** translational symmetry. In how many different directions can you slide the tessellation so it will coincide with itself (ignoring the change in coloring)? (Many students will suggest two directions.) Since any horse can coincide with any other horse in the infinite tessellation, there must be an infinite number of directions possible.*

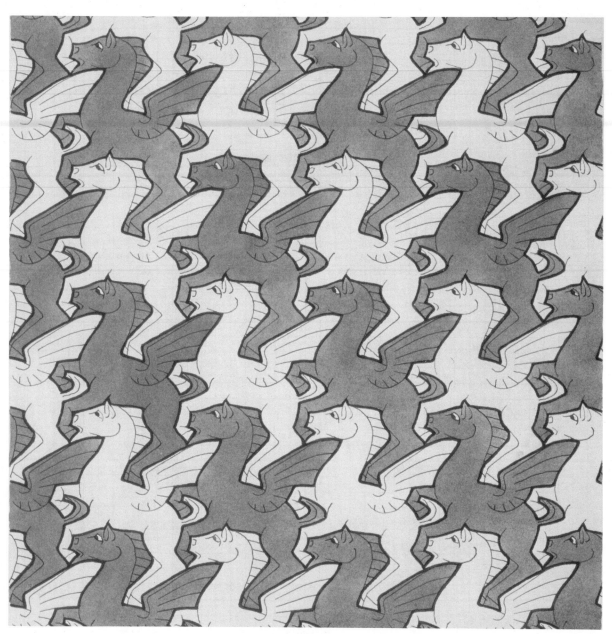

Symmetry Drawing E 105 ©1959 M. C. Escher Heirs / Cordon Art–Baarn–Holland

Transparency 18

Overlay

Student Tessellation (Square)

Assembly Instructions

Color the modified square on the transparency base. As before, this will emphasize that figure and the equivalence of the areas of the original and modified figures.

Commentary

Show the transparency base.

> *We will now use the same procedure to create another non-polygonal tessellating shape.*
>
> *There are two ways to approach our modification of a polygon to create a non-polygonal tessellating shape. One way is to have some specific object in mind—such as with Escher's horse—and to modify the sides of the polygon until its contour resembles that object. A second approach is to modify the sides of the polygon with random curves, then to interpret the resulting shape by adding details to highlight its interior.*
>
> *To create this tessellating shape, the student artist modified a square by translation with no specific object in mind.*

Add the LH overlay.

> *The modified square was first interpreted as a witch . . .*

Remove the LH overlay. Rotate the transparency counterclockwise 90°, then add the RH overlay.

> *. . . and then, with the shape rotated 90°, as a winged seahorse.*

LH Overlay

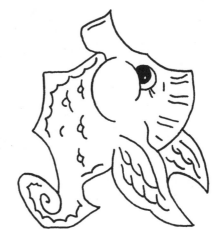

RH Overlay

Student Tessellations
(Rectangle, Parallelogram,
Regular Hexagon)

Assembly Instructions

Transparency 20 and Transparency 21 have a *horizontal format;* the longer edges of the film are oriented horizontally during projection.

Color the modified polygon on each transparency.

Commentary

Any quadrilateral having parallel and congruent sides can be modified by translating the modification of one side to the opposite side.

Show Transparency 20.

"Ferocious Fish" is based on a rectangle, . . .

Show Transparency 21.

. . . while "Demon Elephant" is based on a parallelogram.

Show Transparency 22.

We can extend this method to include regular hexagons. Of course, in this case we have three sets of opposite sides to modify.

Point out each set of parallel modifications.

In these examples, as will be the case with all non-polygonal tessellations that follow, the modified polygon has the same area as the parent polygon.

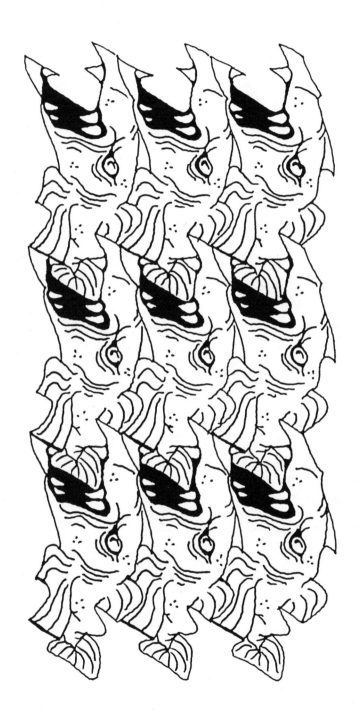

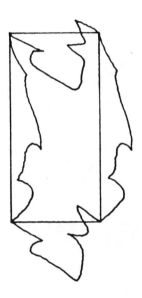

Transparency 20

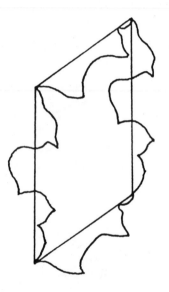

Transparency 21

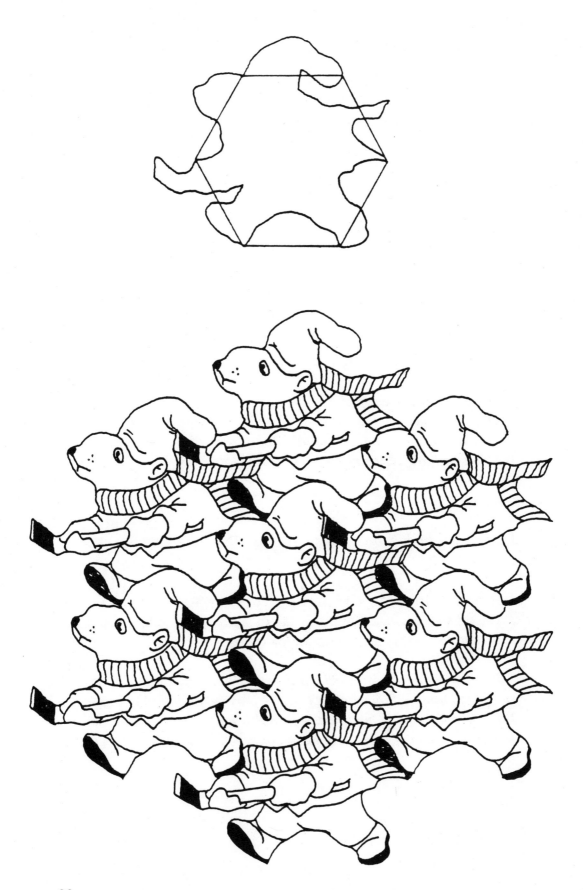

Transparency 22

Modifying by Rotation about the Midpoint of a Side

Assembly Instructions

Process the pieces of overlay.

   Color the figure on Transparency 24 and on its piece of overlay with the same color.

Commentary

The other transformations can also be used to modify polygons to create non-polygonal tessellating shapes.

Show the base of Transparency 23.

Any quadrilateral will tessellate the plane if we rotate the polygon 180° about the midpoint of each of its sides.

Add the overlay.

Suppose we modify this quadrilateral by adding a bump on one of its half sides.

Place the modification on the piece of overlay to coincide with the modification on the overlay. Press the tip of a sharp pencil to the marked point to anchor the two layers. Rotate the piece of overlay 180°.

When we rotate the quadrilateral about the midpoint of that side, the bump will accompany it. We can locate the matching hole by rotating the modification 180° about that midpoint. A bump on one half side becomes a congruent hole on the other half side.

Show Transparency 24.

The modified quadrilateral has the same area as the parent quadrilateral.

Place the modified quadrilateral on the piece of overlay to coincide with the modified quadrilateral on the transparency. Press the tip of a sharp pencil to the midpoint of the modified side to anchor the two layers. Rotate the piece of overlay 180°.

If we rotate the shape 180° about the midpoint of the modified side, the modifications fit together exactly. The modified quadrilateral will tessellate the plane in the same way as the parent quadrilateral.

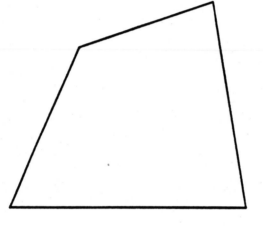

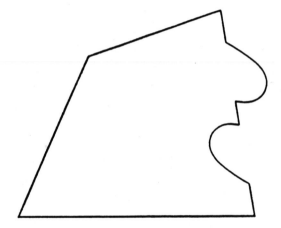

Transparency 24

Modifying by Rotation about Midpoints of Sides

Assembly Instructions

Color the figure on the base of Transparency 25. Make two copies of Transparency 26.

Commentary

Show Transparency 25 with its LH overlay in place.

> *All four sides of this scalene quadrilateral have been modified.*

Circumnavigate the figure with a pointer, starting at the upper right-hand vertex.

> *If we add a bump on one half side, then we must remove a matching hole on the other half side. Add a bump . . . remove a hole. Remove a hole . . . add a bump. Remove a hole . . . add a bump. The resulting modified quadrilateral has the same area as the parent quadrilateral.*

Remove the LH overlay, then add the RH overlay.

> *If we remove the underlying polygon, and add a few interpreting details, we have a non-polygonal tessellating shape. The resulting tessellation, though simple, is quite remarkable.*

Show one copy of Transparency 26. Superimpose the second copy on the first. Slide the upper layer in various directions until one tessellating shape coincides with another.

> *It has translational symmetry.*

Press the tip of a pencil to the center of each distinct modified side. Rotate the upper layer 180° until a tessellating shape again coincides with another.

> *It also has 2-fold rotational symmetry about the midpoint of each of its modified sides—just like the scalene quadrilateral tessellation that was its basis.*

Base

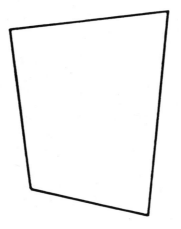

Transparency 26

Student Tessellations
(Scalene Quadrilaterals)

Assembly Instructions

Transparency 31 has a horizontal format.

Color the modified quadrilateral on each transparency base.

Commentary

Given the enormous variety of quadrilaterals, we can use rotation about midpoints of sides to create a wealth of non-polygonal tessellating shapes.

For each transparency, show the base. Ask the students if they can identify the shape or give it a meaning. Then add the overlay.

In Transparency 27, circumnavigate the tessellating shape, pointing out the fit. You might make a duplicate of the shape and use it like a piece of overlay to confirm the 180° rotations.

In Transparency 28, the parent quadrilateral is a square. So far, we have learned two totally different ways of modifying a square.

In Transparency 29, ask which bumps correspond to which holes—particularly along the upper side. Remark on the fact that two dogs share a bow tie.

In Transparency 30, most students will identify the deer or elk head as such. The student artist painstakingly modified the sides of the quadrilateral until its contour resembled that object. Comment on how the antlers intertwine and how the bulge on one of the antlers fits in the deer's mouth.

In Transparency 31, comment on how the wart on the pirate's nose fits in his mouth.

When students begin to create their own non-polygonal tessellating shapes, they seem to gravitate naturally towards modifying scalene quadrilaterals. The very nature of a scalene quadrilateral tessellation allows them to alter the sides and angles of the parent polygon at will—a freedom they will not be allowed with any other polygon except a scalene triangle. Of course, the underlying quadrilateral tessellation is harder to construct that a regular one—but that doesn't seem to discourage them.

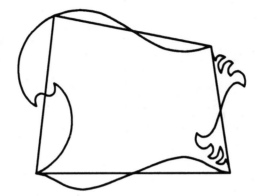

Base

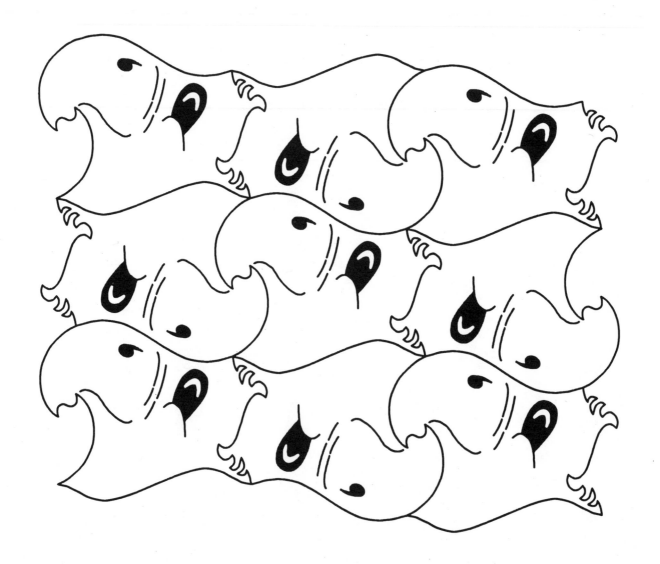

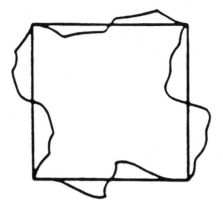

Base

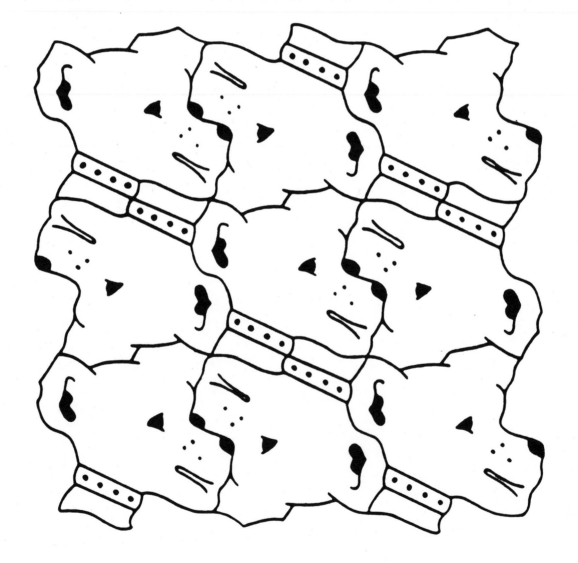

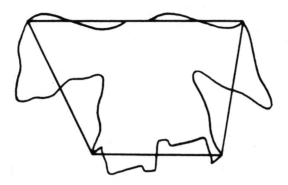

Base

Base

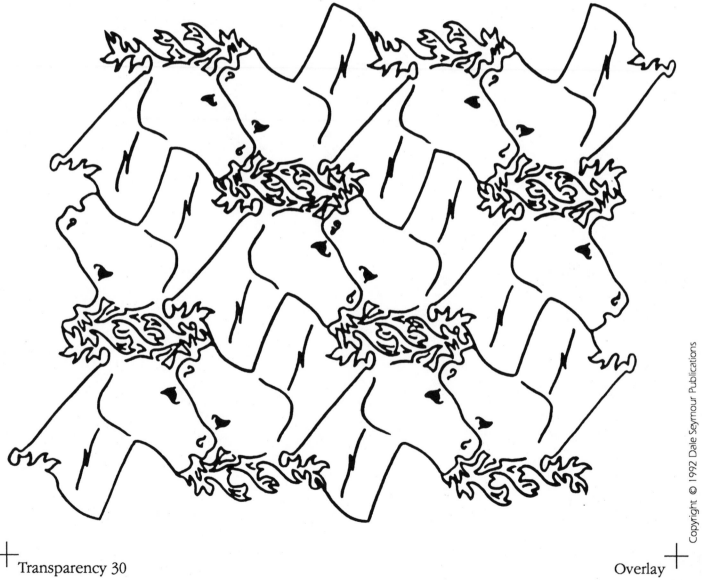

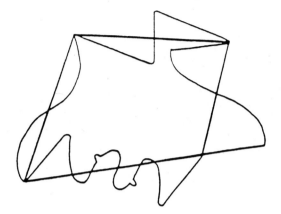

Base

Student Tessellations
(Scalene Triangles)

Assembly Instructions

Color the modified triangle on each transparency.

Commentary

Show Transparency 32, then Transparency 33.

> *We can use rotation about the midpoints of sides on any triangle as well.*
>
> *Here are two examples of tessellating shapes created by modifying each half side of a triangle and rotating the modification 180° about the midpoint of the side. Can you find the three different centers of 2-fold rotation in each design?*

You might mention that modifying by rotation about midpoints of sides cannot be used to modify regular hexagons—or ask the students to find out for themselves by experimentation. If they don't use the *same* modification on each half side, they will be in serious trouble!

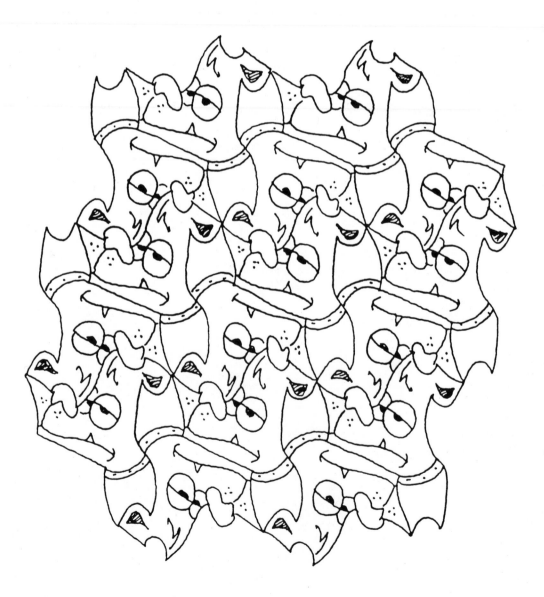

Transparency 32

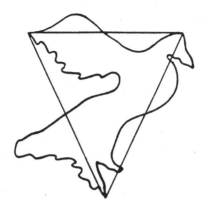

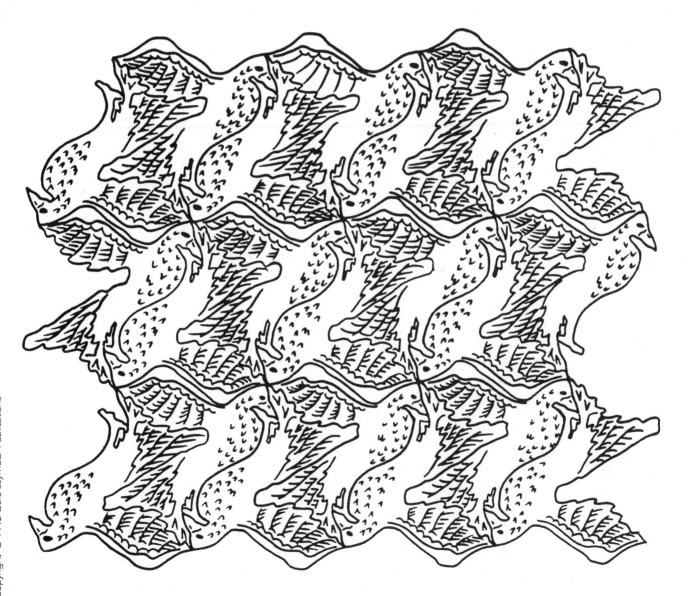

Transparency 33

"Lizard I"

Assembly Instructions

Make two copies of the transparency base, using green colored-on-clear film.

Commentary

Show the transparency base.

Now let's consider a somewhat more complex Escher tessellation.

Superimpose the second copy of "Lizard I" on the first. Slide the upper layer in a variety of directions until a lizard coincides with a lizard.

Like "Pegasus," this tessellation has translational symmetry. A lizard can be made to coincide with a lizard of the same or opposite color by a simple translation in some direction.

*The tessellation also has rotational symmetry. One way of locating centers of rotation is to circumnavigate the tessellating shape, looking for points at which **more than two** shapes meet. Exactly four lizards meet at each lizard's right "elbow," the extreme tip of its right leg, its left knee, and the extreme tip of its left "arm." Each of these points is a center of 2-fold rotation.*

Press the tip of a sharp pencil to each center of rotation to anchor the two layers. Show that a lizard can be made to coincide with an adjacent lizard of the same color by a 180° rotation about any of these points. Add overlay 1.

On the same lizard, these four centers of rotation mark the vertices of a parallelogram. The midpoints of the two shorter sides are also centers of 2-fold rotation. Adjacent lizards of opposite color can be made to coincide by a 180° rotation about either of these midpoints.

Confirm this statement as above. Then add overlay 2.

The basis of the tessellation is a grid of parallelograms. Each lizard fits in its parent parallelogram in exactly the same way as its fellow lizards.

Symmetry Drawing E 75 ©1949 M. C. Escher Heirs / Cordon Art–Baarn–Holland

Transparency 34

Overlay 2

"Lizard I" Tessellating Shape

Assembly Instructions

Color the modified square on the transparency base—preferably green.

Commentary

Show the transparency base.

> *If we study the contour of a lizard inscribed in its parent parallelogram, we find we can create this tessellating shape by a combination of translation and rotation about midpoints of sides.*

Add the overlay.

> *The sides of the parallelogram are numbered for reference. First, a modification to side 2 is translated to side 4. Then, modifications to half of side 1 and half of side 3 are rotated 180° about the midpoints of those sides.*

Point out corresponding bumps and holes for each of these modifications.

> *Because more than one kind of modification is involved in this procedure, we shall introduce a convenient notation to present these changes in symbolic form. Can you "read" the symbols?*

Point to the notation at the top of the overlay. The notation is not essential to the discussion, but it is convenient and unambiguous. Use it at your own discretion. Then return Transparency 34 without the overlays in place. Point to the corresponding lizards as per the commentary.

> *Modification by translation is manifested in the slanted rows of identically oriented lizards. Modification by rotation about midpoints of sides causes the 180° change in orientation between these rows. The four centers of 2-fold rotation that mark the vertices of the parent parallelogram were not planned for in the modifying procedure, but natural consequences of it.*

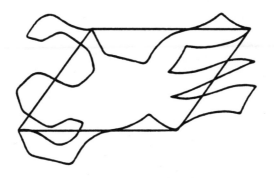

$2 \longleftrightarrow 4$ $1 \overset{\bullet}{\longleftrightarrow} 1$ $3 \overset{\bullet}{\longleftrightarrow} 3$

2

1   3

4

Overlay

Student Tessellation (Rectangle)

Assembly Instructions

Process the piece of overlay.
The transparency has a horizontal format. Color the modified rectangle.

Commentary

We can use translation to one parallel set of sides of a parallelogram and rotation about the midpoints of the other two sides to create our own non-polygonal tessellating shape.

Show the transparency.

Here the parallelogram used by the student artist is a rectangle. The shape can be interpreted as a rabbit or, . . .

Rotate the transparency 180°. Place the bulldog on the piece of overlay to coincide with the modified rectangle on the transparency.

. . . if we rotate it 180°, as a bulldog with a snappy bow tie.

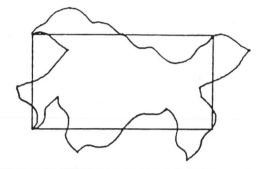

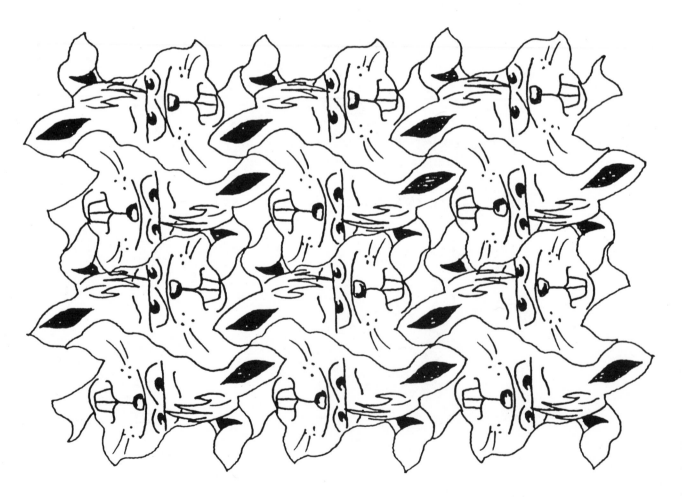

Transparency 36

"Lizard II"

Assembly Instructions

Make two copies of the transparency base, using green colored-on-clear film.

Commentary

Show the transparency base.

> *This Escher tessellation of lizards has both translational and rotational symmetry.*

Superimpose the second copy of "Lizard II" on the first.

> *As before, we will look for centers of rotation to locate the vertices of the underlying grid. Can you locate any such points? (Exactly four lizards meet at each lizard's nose, right front foot, right knee and left rear foot. Each lizard's nose and right knee is a center of 2-fold rotation. Ignoring color differences, its right front foot and left rear foot are centers of 4-fold rotation.)*

Press the tip of a sharp pencil to each center of rotation to anchor the two layers. Show that a lizard can be made to coincide with an adjacent lizard by an appropriate rotation (180° or 90°) about any of these points.

> *On the same lizard, these four centers of rotation mark the vertices of a square.*

Add the overlay.

> *The tessellation is based on a grid of squares. Each lizard fits in its parent square in exactly the same way as its fellow lizards.*

Symmetry Drawing E 104 ©1959 M. C. Escher Heirs / Cordon Art–Baarn–Holland

Transparency 37

Overlay

"Lizard II" Tessellating Shape

Assembly Instructions

Process the piece of overlay.

Color the modified square on the transparency base and on the piece of overlay with the same color—preferably green.

Commentary

If we study the contour of a lizard inscribed in its parent square, we find that we can create this tessellating shape by rotating modifications to sides of the square about its vertices.

Add the overlay.

Suppose we number the sides and letter the vertices of the square for reference.

Place the figure on the piece of overlay to coincide with the figure on the transparency base. Press the tip of a sharp pencil to the vertex labelled *A* to anchor the piece of overlay. Then turn the piece of overlay counterclockwise 90° until the modifications again coincide. Repeat for the vertex labelled *C*.

First, a modification to side 1 has been rotated 90° about vertex A to side 2. As a result, a bump on side 1 becomes a congruent hole on side 2, and vice versa. In the same way, a modification to side 3 has been rotated 90° about vertex C to side 4.

Because rotation about a vertex is yet another way of modifying a polygon, we shall introduce a convenient notation that presents these changes in symbolic form. Can you read the symbols?

Point to the notation at the top of the overlay. As before, use the notation at your discretion.

With these modifications in mind, we will find that the generation of the corresponding tessellation is far easier than its many symmetries suggest.

Return Transparency 37 without the overlay in place. (If the absence of the underlying grid causes difficulties for the students, add the overlay.) Superimpose the second copy of "Lizard II" on the first.

Point to the complete dark lizard oriented like the tessellating shape just considered and located in the upper left-hand portion of the tessellation. Press the tip of a sharp pencil to the center of rotation located at the lizard's left rear foot to anchor the two layers. Rotate the upper layer through successive increments of 90° until it returns to its starting position.

Starting with any lizard, we can generate the tessellation simply by rotating the shape 90° four times about a center of 4-fold rotation (vertex A or vertex C) until it returns to its original position, . . .

Slide the upper layer to the right until the two layers again coincide and repeat the rotations. Then slide the upper layer downward and repeat.

. . . then translating it two positions, or "squares," both horizontally and vertically, and repeating the process.

The centers of 2-fold rotation that mark the other two vertices of the parent square (vertex B and vertex D) were not planned for in the modifying procedure, but natural consequences of it.

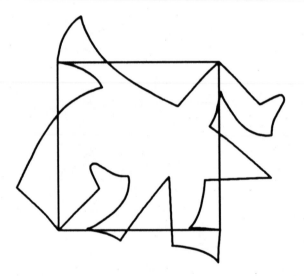

1 ⟵A⟶ 2   3 ⟵C⟶ 4

A   2   B

1   3

D   4   C

Modifying by Rotation about
Vertices of a Square

Assembly Instructions

Color the figure on the base of Transparency 39.

For Transparency 40, use black-on-clear film or black-on-colored film whose background is the same color as on Transparency 39.

Commentary

Show Transparency 39 with its LH overlay in place.

> *The same procedure—modifying by rotation about opposite vertices of a square—was used to create this tessellating shape. We started with a bird in mind and modified the sides of the square until its contour resembled a bird with wings outspread.*

Point out the corresponding bumps and holes. Remove the LH overlay, then add the RH overlay.

> *With the addition of a few details, the interpretation is reinforced.*

Show Transparency 40.

> *The resulting tessellation has two different centers of 4-fold rotation and two different centers of 2-fold rotation, just like the Escher tessellation whose pattern inspired it.*

Ask the students to point out the various centers of rotation, and to classify them as 4-fold or 2-fold.

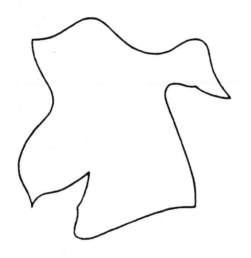

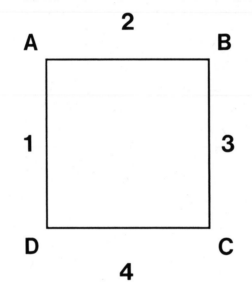

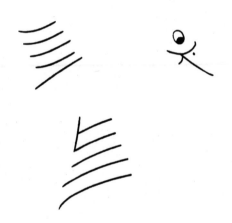

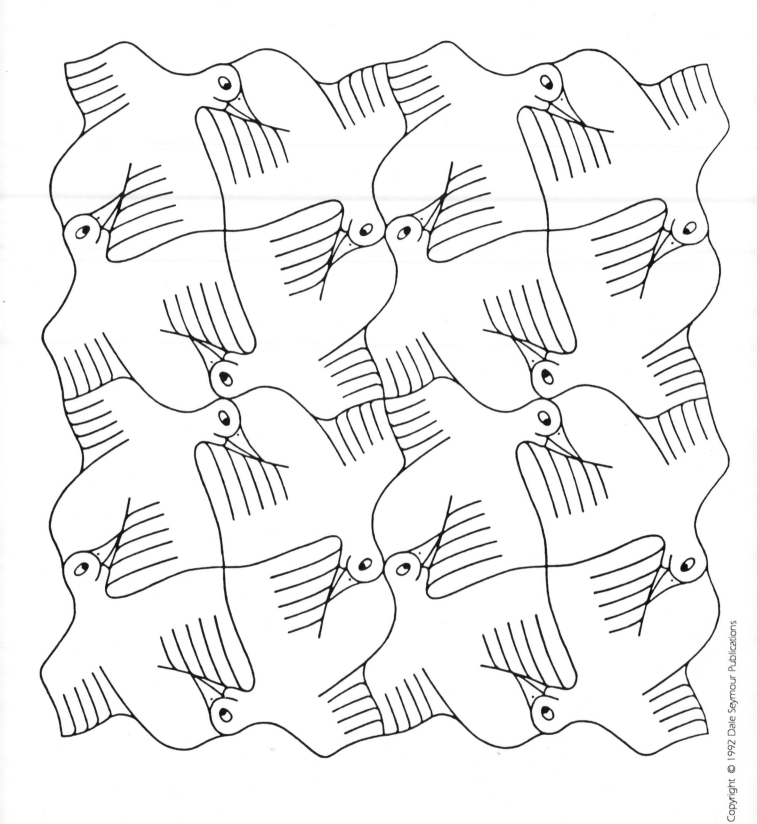

Transparency 40

Student Tessellations (Square)

Assembly Instructions

Color the modified square on each transparency.

Commentary

Show Transparency 41.

> *Here are two more examples of tessellating shapes that result from rotating modifications about vertices of a square. In creating each of these, the student artist made random modifications to the vertical sides of a square, then rotated each modification to the adjacent side about either the upper left or bottom right vertex.*

> *He interpreted this shape as a goofy moose, . . .*

Show Transparency 42.

> *. . . and this one as a rogue or scoundrel with a plumed hat.*

Mention that the rotations could just as easily have been about the upper right and bottom left hand vertices—as long as the vertices are opposite one another or, more generally, as long as they are **alternate** vertices.

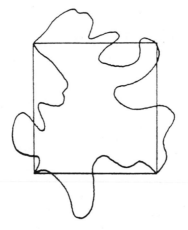

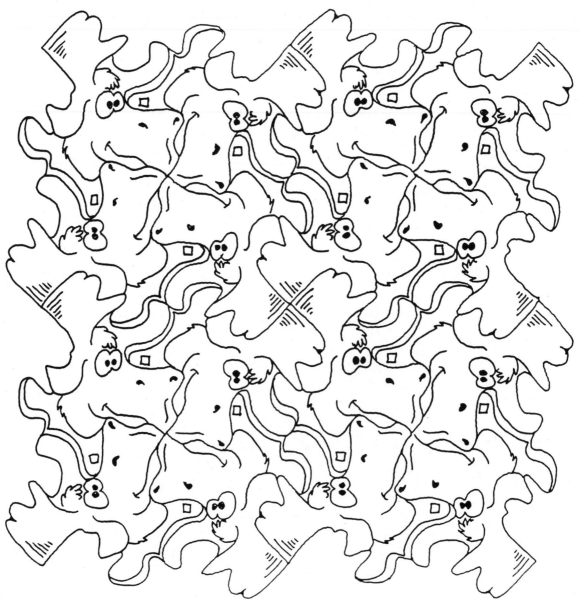

Transparency 41

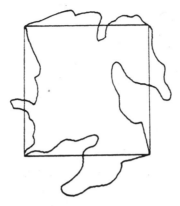

Transparency 42

"Reptiles"

Assembly Instructions

The transparency has a horizontal format. Process using a photocopy method.

Commentary

Show the transparency.

Escher left notebooks filled with studies and sketches of repeating patterns, many of which he incorporated into woodcuts and lithographs. One such lithograph, "Reptiles," shows an intrepid lizard crawling out of Escher's two-dimensional sketch to explore the real world before rejoining his fellow reptiles in the interlocking design.

If you examine the tessellation, you will notice a grid of regular hexagons superimposed on it. Even though the reptiles are turning this way and that, each fits in its hexagon in exactly the same way.

Reptiles ©1943 M. C. Escher Heirs / Cordon Art–Baarn–Holland

Transparency 43

"Reptiles" Tessellating Shape

Assembly Instructions

Process the piece of overlay.

Color the modified hexagon on the transparency and on the piece of overlay with the same color—preferably green.

Commentary

Show the transparency.

> *If we study the contour of a lizard inscribed in its parent hexagon, we find that we can create this tessellating shape by rotating modifications to sides of the regular hexagon about its vertices.*

Place the figure on the piece of overlay to coincide with the figure on the transparency. Press the tip of a sharp pencil to each rotation point to anchor the piece of overlay. Then turn the piece clockwise or counterclockwise 120° until the modifications again coincide.

> *Modifications to alternate sides have been rotated 120° about alternate vertices. A bump on a side becomes a congruent hole on the adjacent side, and vice versa.*

You might ask the students how they could represent the modifications using the previously established notation (see *Introduction to Tessellations*, p. 207). It serves no advantageous purpose here and can actually detract from an understanding of the nature of the modifications (alternate sides/alternate vertices).

Transparency 44

"Study of Regular Division of the Plane with Reptiles"

Assembly Instructions

Make two copies of the transparency base using a photocopy method. To guarantee alignment, use the same photocopy method for the overlay.

Commentary

Show the transparency.

> *This lizard shape tessellates in a pattern with three different centers of 3-fold rotational symmetry—in addition to the usual translational symmetry.*

Superimpose the second copy of the tessellation on the first. Point to an appropriate white lizard (which will be oriented like the tessellating shape just considered).

Press the tip of a sharp pencil to each center of rotation to anchor the two layers. Rotate the upper layer through successive increments of 120° until it returns to its starting position. If the students have trouble locating the centers of rotation, add the overlay.

> *A rotation of 120° about any of these points will bring the design into coincidence. Starting with any lizard, we can generate the tessellation simply by rotating the shape 120° three times about a center of 3-fold rotation until it returns to its original position, . . .*

Slide the upper layer until a white lizard again coincides with a white lizard.

> *. . . then translating it in an appropriate direction, and repeating the process.*

Symmetry Drawing E 25 ©1939 M. C. Escher Heirs / Cordon Art–Baarn–Holland

Base

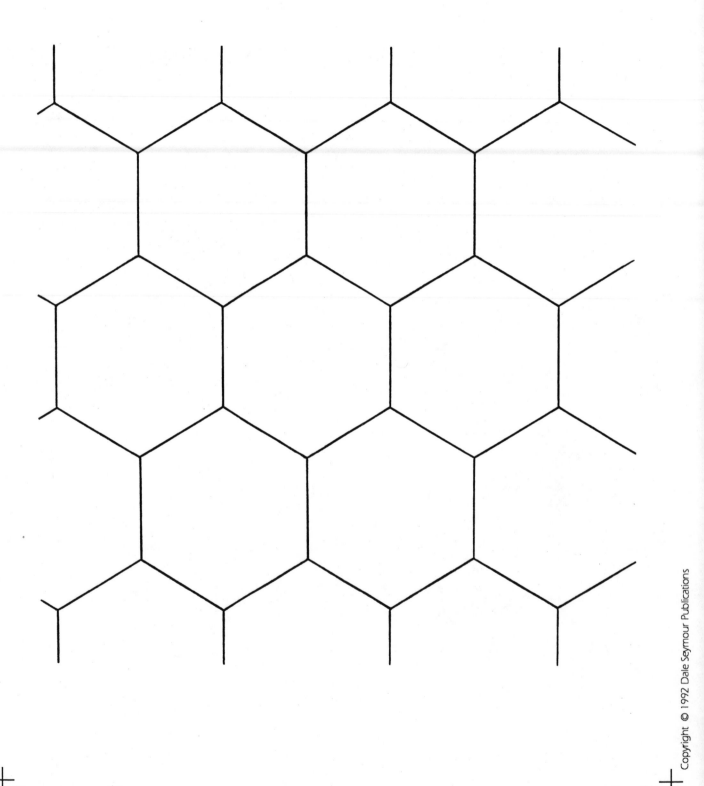

Modifying by Rotation about Vertices of a Regular Hexagon

Assembly Instructions

Color the figure on the base of Transparency 46.

For Transparency 47, use black-on-clear film or black-on-colored film whose background is the same color as on Transparency 46.

Commentary

Show Transparency 46 with its LH overlay in place.

We can use the same procedure—rotating modifications to alternate sides of a regular hexagon about alternate vertices to create our own non-polygonal tessellating shape.

Remove the LH overlay, then add the RH overlay.

The resulting outline resembles a peg-legged pirate, even before we add interior details.

Show Transparency 47.

The resulting tessellation ("War of the Buccaneers") has three different centers of 3-fold rotation. Can you find them?

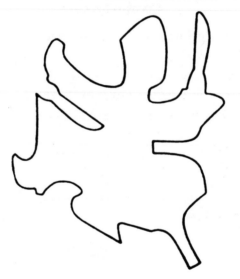

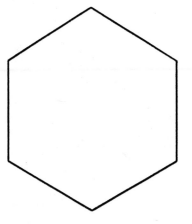

LH Overlay

Transparency 47

Student Tessellation
(Regular Hexagon)

Assembly Instructions

Color the modified hexagon on the base of Transparency 48.

For Transparency 49, use black-on-clear film or black-on-colored film whose background is the same color as on Transparency 48.

Commentary

Show the base of Transparency 48.

> *This tessellating shape was created by the same procedure as the last. The student artist made random modifications to alternate sides of a regular hexagon, then rotated each of them about their right-hand endpoints to the adjacent side.*

Add the overlay.

> *He then gave three different interpretations to the shape—a broad-beaked parrot, a crested bird, and a flying squirrel.*

Show Transparency 49.

> *In the resulting tessellation ("Trouble in Paradise"), identically oriented shapes were given the same interpretation.*

Rotate the transparency 180° for the full effect.

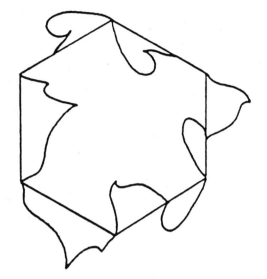

Transparency 49

"Birds"

Assembly Instructions

Make two copies of the transparency base using a photocopy method. To guarantee alignment, use the same photocopy method for the overlay.

Commentary

Show the transparency base.

> *Both rotation procedures—rotation about a vertex of a polygon and rotation about a midpoint of a side of that polygon—were used to create the tessellating shape in Escher's "Birds."*

> *Let's look for centers of rotation as we try to discover the underlying polygonal grid. Can you locate any such points? (Exactly six birds meet at the tip of each bird's beak and at the lower tip of each of its wings. The tip of each bird's beak and the lower tip of its right wing are centers of 3-fold rotation. Ignoring color differences, the lower tip of its left wing is a center of 6-fold rotation.)*

Superimpose the second copy of "Birds" on the first. Press the tip of a sharp pencil to each center of rotation to anchor the two layers. Show that a bird can be made to coincide with an adjacent bird by an appropriate rotation (120° or 60°) about any of these points.

> *On the same bird, these three centers of rotation mark the vertices of an equilateral triangle. The basis of the tessellation is a grid of equilateral triangles.*

Add the overlay. Point to a center of 2-fold rotation (located midway between the beaks of adjacent light and dark birds).

> *Another center of rotation, often overlooked, is located at the midpoint of one of the sides of each triangle. This is a center of 2-fold rotation. A rotation of 180° about any such point will also bring adjacent birds into coincidence.*

Symmetry Drawing E 44 ©1941 M. C. Escher Heirs / Cordon Art–Baarn–Holland

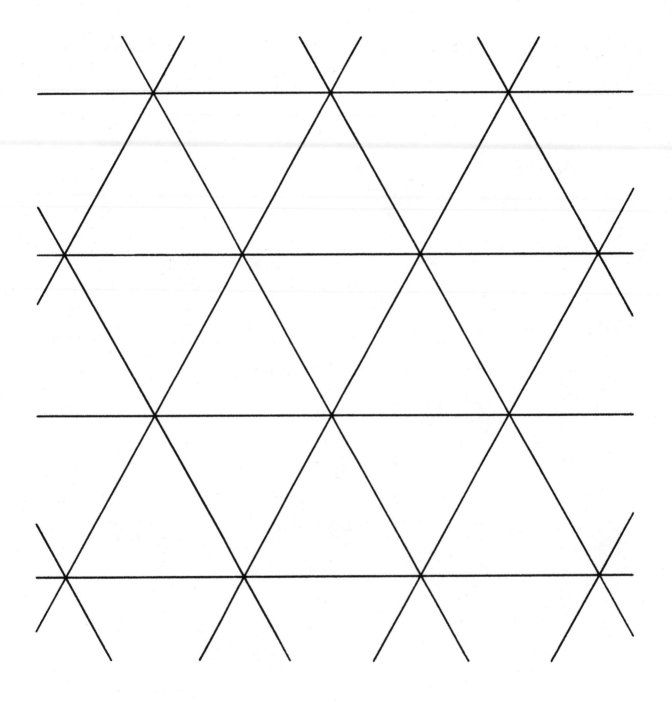

Overlay

"Birds" Tessellating Shape

Assembly Instructions

Process the piece of overlay.

   Color the modified triangle on the transparency base and on the piece of overlay with the same color.

Commentary

Show the transparency base.

> *To discover the modifying procedure, let's study the contour of a single bird inscribed in its parent triangle.*

Add the overlay.

> *For reference, we'll number the sides and letter the vertices of the triangle.*

Place the figure on the piece of overlay to coincide with the figure on the transparency base. Press the tip of a sharp pencil to the vertex labelled **A** to anchor the piece of overlay to the base. Then turn the piece of overlay counterclockwise 60° until the modifications again coincide.

> *First, a modification to side 1 has been rotated 60° about vertex A to side 2. As a result, a bump on side 1 becomes a congruent hole on side 2, and vice versa.*

> *Since a triangle has an odd number of sides, side 3 has no partner, so we cannot continue to use rotation about a vertex. Instead, we modify half of side 3 and rotate the modification 180° about the midpoint of that side. The bird shape is now complete.*

Point to the notation at the top of the overlay.

> *Can you read the symbols that represent this modifying procedure?*

Return Transparency 50 without the overlay in place. (If the absence of the underlying grid causes difficulties for the students, add the overlay.) Superimpose the second copy of "Birds" on the first.

Point to a bird near the center of the tessellation. Press the tip of a sharp pencil to the center of rotation located at its left wing tip to anchor the two layers. Rotate the upper layer through successive increments of 60° until the bird returns to its starting position.

> *Starting with any bird, we can generate the tessellation simply by rotating the shape 60° six times about the center of 6-fold rotation that marks its left wing tip until it returns to its original position, . . .*

Fix the tip of the pencil to the corresponding center of 2-fold rotation. Rotate the upper layer through 180° until the two layers again coincide.

> *. . . then rotating it 180° about the center of 2-fold rotation that marks the midpoint of the opposite side of the corresponding triangle. The process is then repeated with the bird in this inverted position.*

> *The centers of 3-fold rotation that mark the other two vertices of the parent triangle (vertex B and vertex C) were not planned for in the modifying procedure, but natural consequences of it.*

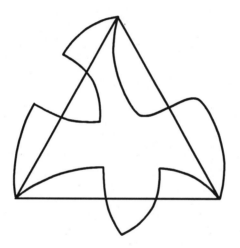

Transparency 51

Base

1 ⤴ A ⤵ 2   3 ⤴ • ⤵ 3

B

2   3

A   C

1

Modifying by Rotation in an Equilateral Triangle

Assembly Instructions

Color the figure on the base of Transparency 52.

For Transparency 53, use black-on-clear film or black-on-colored film whose background is the same color as on Transparency 52.

Commentary

Show Transparency 52 with its LH overlay in place.

> *The same combination of procedures—modifying by rotation about a vertex of an equilateral triangle and modifying by rotation about the midpoint of the opposite side—was used to create this tessellating shape. Can you see the changes?*

Point out the corresponding bumps and holes. Remove the LH overlay, then add the RH overlay.

> *The random shape was interpreted by the student artist as a dog with a rather prominent nose at vertex A.*

Show Transparency 53.

> *The resulting tessellation has an obvious center of 6-fold rotation where these noses meet, as would be expected. It also has centers of 3-fold and 2-fold rotation, as did the Escher tessellation that inspired it. Can you find them?*

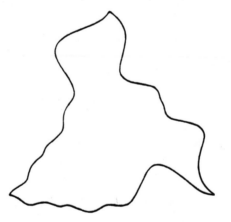

Transparency 52

Base

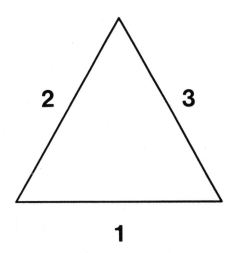

Transparency 53

Student Tessellation
(Equilateral Triangle)

Assembly Instructions

Color the modified triangle on the base of Transparency 54.

For Transparency 55, use black-on-clear film or black-on-colored film whose background is the same color as on Transparency 54. Reverse image film, preferably yellow on green or red, is also very effective.

Commentary

Show the base of Transparency 54.

This tessellating shape was created by the same combination of procedures—modifying by rotation about a vertex of an equilateral triangle and modifying by rotation about the midpoint of the opposite side. The student artist made random modifications to an equilateral triangle, . . .

Add the overlay.

. . . then experimented with six different interpretations: a duck, a bird, a mutant horse, a goblin, a dragon, and a cuckoo.

Show Transparency 55.

Here we see the dragon tessellating. Can you find centers of rotational symmetry?

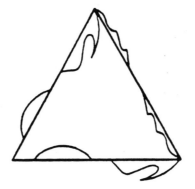

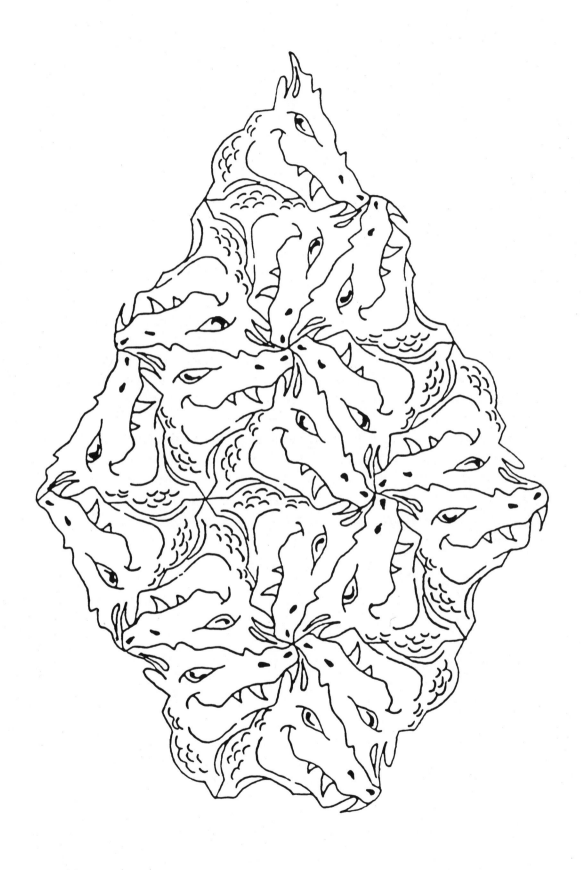

Transparency 55

"Lizard IV" Tessellating Shape

Assembly Instructions

Color the modified triangle on the transparency.

Commentary

Show the transparency.

> *The same combination of procedures was used by Escher to create this tessellating shape. The underlying polygon is an isosceles right triangle. Because the apex angle is 90°, rather than the previous 60° of an equilateral triangle, the modified triangle will be rotated four times about vertex A.*

> *You may wonder why the modified triangle will tessellate. When the shape is rotated about vertex A, the underlying triangle generates a square. Any quadrilateral can be modified by rotation about the midpoints of each of its sides. In this case, the same modification has been made to each half side of the square.*

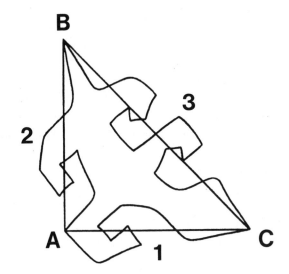

"Lizard IV"

Assembly Instructions

Make two copies of the transparency base using a photocopy method. To guarantee alignment, use the same photocopy method for the overlay.

Commentary

Show the transparency base, then add the overlay.

> *As would be expected, the resulting tessellation has a center of 4-fold rotation at the vertex of the right angle and a center of 2-fold rotation at the midpoint of the hypotenuse. As a natural consequence, it also has a center of 4-fold rotation at each base vertex (vertex B and vertex C), where the heads of either four light or four dark lizards meet.*

If the situation merits it, remove the overlay and use the duplicate of the transparency base to confirm these observations.

Symmetry Drawing E 35 ©1941 M. C. Escher Heirs / Cordon Art–Baarn–Holland

Base

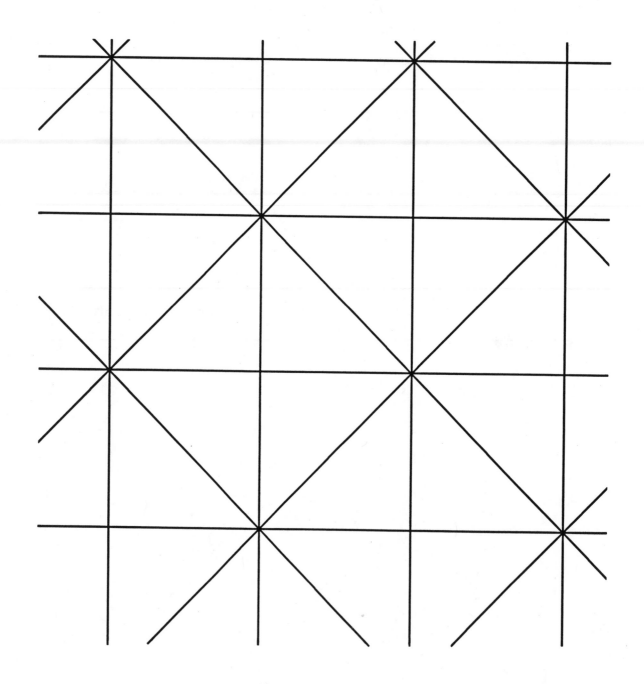

120° Isosceles Triangle Tessellation

Assembly Instructions

Color the modified triangle on Transparency 58.

For Transparency 59, use black-on-clear film or black-on-colored film whose background is the same color as on Transparency 58. Reverse image film is also very effective.

Commentary

Show Transparency 58.

We can use the same combination of procedures as before—modifying by rotation about the apex angle of an isosceles triangle and modifying by rotation about the midpoint of the opposite side—to modify an isosceles triangle with an apex angle of 120°.

The underlying triangle will generate an equilateral triangle when it is rotated three times about vertex A. Any triangle can also be modified by rotation about the midpoints of each of its sides. The same modification has simply been made to each half side.

Show Transparency 59. Use a pointer to indicate the centers of rotation as per the commentary.

The resulting tessellation of hummingbirds has 3-fold rotational symmetry at those points that mark the apex of the underlying triangle—as opposed to 6-fold when we start with an equilateral triangle or 4-fold when we use an isosceles right triangle.

There is the expected center of 2-fold rotation at those points that mark the midpoint of the base of the underlying triangle. It also has a center of 6-fold rotation. Can you find it?

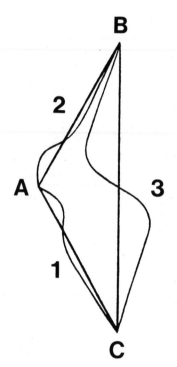

Transparency 58

Transparency 59

"Metamorphosis 1"

Assembly Instructions

The transparency has a horizontal format. Use a photocopy method for the base.

Color the left half of the human figure on the overlay.

Commentary

Show the transparency base.

> *The underlying polygon for the human figure at the right side of Escher's "Metamorphosis 1" woodcut . . .*

Add the overlay.

> *. . . is also a 120° isosceles triangle. A modification to one leg of the triangle has been rotated 120° about the vertex at its apex to the other leg—just like in the preceding tessellation. In this case, however, the figure has been flipped about the base of the triangle—rather than being further modified by a rotation about the midpoint of that side.*

> *The resulting tessellation, which we can see metamorphosing or evolving out of an Italian landscape, has reflective symmetry as well as the expected 3-fold rotational symmetry and the usual translational symmetry.*

Base

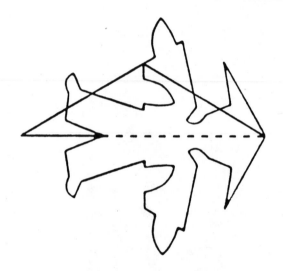

Modifying by Rotation about a Vertex and Reflection

Assembly Instructions

Color the modified triangle on Transparency 61.

Transparency 62 is quite effective if you take the time to color the clowns' mouths, noses and pompons with red color-projecting adhesive film and their hats with a contrasting color, say blue. (You may wish to color the clown face on Transparency 2 in the same way.)

Commentary

Show Transparency 61.

The same isosceles triangle and the same modifying procedures were used to create this tessellating shape.

A modification to side 1 was rotated 120° about vertex A to side 2. The tessellating shape will be reflected about side 3. Can you read the symbols?

Show the transparency.

The resulting clown face tessellates in a pattern that has translational symmetry, reflective symmetry, and 3-fold rotational symmetry about the upper tip of either of its perfectly matched ears.

3 ┊ 3

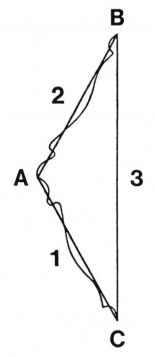

Transparency 62

"Crabs"

Assembly Instructions

Make two copies of the transparency base using a photocopy method. To guarantee alignment, use the same photocopy method for the overlay.

Commentary

Show the transparency base.

> *The tessellating element for this Escher tessellation of crabs was also created by a combination of transformations that includes reflection.*

> *Each point at which four **(more than two)** crabs meet is a center of 2-fold rotation.*

Use the second copy of "Crabs" to investigate these centers of rotation. Then add the overlay.

> *If we draw horizontal and vertical lines through these centers of rotation—then add the obvious vertical lines of reflection—we find that the design is based on a grid of rectangles. One crab half fits in its rectangle in exactly the same way as all the other corresponding crab halves.*

> *The tessellation has reflective symmetry and the usual translational symmetry. Any tessellation with both translational and reflective symmetry will also have glide-reflection symmetry. Ignoring color differences, the tessellation can be made to coincide with itself by reflecting it about any mirror line and then translating it vertically.*

Symmetry Drawing E 117 ©1963 M. C. Escher Heirs / Cordon Art–Baarn–Holland

Base

"Crabs" Tessellating Shape

Assembly Instructions

Color the modified rectangle on the transparency base.

Commentary

Show the transparency base.

> *If we study the contour of a single crab half inscribed in its parent rectangle, we see that a modification to side 2 has been translated to side 4. We also find that side 1 has been modified by rotation about its midpoint. In the tessellation, the former transformation is manifested in the rows of identically oriented crabs and the latter in the 180° change in orientation between these rows. The shape is reflected about side 3. You can see how the corresponding notation is particularly useful here.*

You might return Transparency 63 as you point out these effects. Use the copy of the tessellation to confirm the center of 2-fold rotation at the midpoint of a side of a parent rectangle. Point out that the centers of 2-fold rotation at the vertices of the rectangle are merely natural consequences of the modifying procedure.

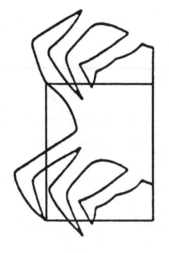

2  **4**   **1**  **1**   **3** ┊ **3**

2

1   **3**

4

Student Tessellation (Rectangle)

Assembly Instructions

Color the modified rectangle on Transparency 65 red.
For Transparency 66, use black-on-clear film or red black-on-colored film.

Commentary

Show Transparency 65.

> *The same combination of modifying procedures has been used to create this tessellating shape—translation between sides 2 and 4, rotation about the midpoint of side 1, and reflection about side 3.*

Show Transparency 66.

> *The shape suggested a devilish visage to the student artist. The resulting pattern has translational symmetry, reflective symmetry, glide-reflection symmetry, and 2-fold rotational symmetry—just like the Escher tessellation that inspired it.*

2 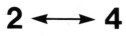 **4**   **1**  **1**   **3**  **3**

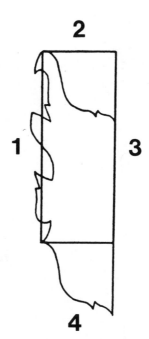

2

1   3

4

Transparency 66

"Dogs"

Assembly Instructions

Make two copies of the transparency base, using colored-on-clear film. Use black-on-clear film or colored-on-clear film of a contrasting color for the overlays.

Commentary

Show the transparency base.

> *This tessellation of dogs is one of Escher's most ingenious designs. Note how the black dogs' rear toes become teeth for the white dogs, and vice versa.*

> *The tessellation has translational symmetry—as did all of its predecessors.*

Use the second copy of "Dogs" to examine the translational symmetry. Concentrate on horizontal and vertical translations, ignoring color differences in the process. Then add the LH overlay.

> *If we were to reflect the tessellation about any of the vertical lines shown, then translate it vertically downward, a white dog would exchange places with the black dog just below it, and vice versa. If color is ignored, the tessellation has glide-reflection symmetry. It does not have reflective symmetry.*

You can attempt to use the duplicate of the tessellation to investigate the glide-reflection symmetry but the effect is generally unsatisfactory. The nature of the transformation will be clarified in Transparency 68.
Remove the LH overlay.

> *In Escher's tessellations with rotational symmetry, we discovered that centers of rotation at which **more than two** tessellating shapes meet will mark the vertices of the underlying polygonal grid.*

*Although this tessellation lacks rotational symmetry, suppose we again look for points at which **more than two** tessellating shapes meet. Exactly four dogs meet at the tip of each dog's chin—a point that also marks the tip of either a front or rear paw, or the middle of the back of adjacent dogs.*

Circumnavigate a typical dog two or three times with your pointer, calling attention to the above points en route.

On the same dog, these points mark the vertices of a parallelogram.

Add the RH overlay.

The basis of the tessellation is a grid of parallelograms in two different orientations. Each dog fits in its parent parallelogram in the same way as its fellow dogs.

We have discovered a way of revealing the grid that is the basis of a tessellation, a method that is applicable whether or not that tessellation has rotational symmetry.

Symmetry Drawing E 97 ©1955 M. C. Escher Heirs / Cordon Art–Baarn–Holland

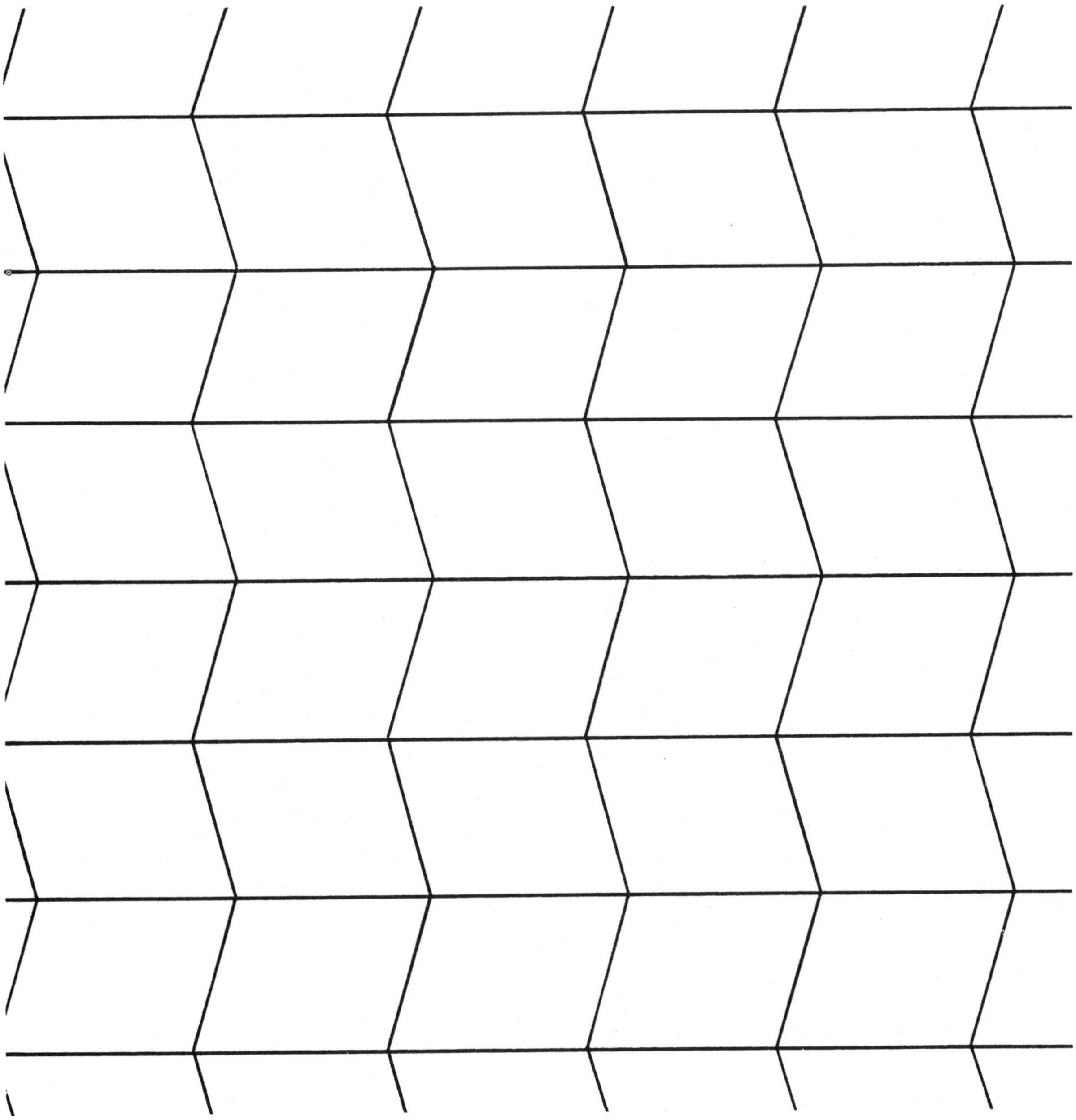

"Dogs" Tessellating Shape

Assembly Instructions

Process the piece of overlay.

Color the modified parallelogram on the transparency base and on the piece of overlay with the same color.

Commentary

Show the transparency base.

Let's study the contour of a single dog inscribed in its parent parallelogram.

Add overlay 1.

As before, we'll number the sides of the polygon for reference. First, a modification to side 1 has been translated to side 3. In the tessellation, this transformation is manifested in the horizontal rows of identically oriented dogs.

Use the piece on overlay to confirm the horizontal translation, then add overlay 2. Place the figure on the piece of overlay to coincide with the figure on the transparency base. Lift the piece of overlay, then flip it about the vertical line. When you reposition it, the subsequent vertical translation should result in coincidence of the modifications.

Then, a modification to side 2 is reflected about the vertical line that passes through the center of the parallelogram, ...

Slide the piece of overlay vertically downward.

... and the reflected modification is translated vertically to side 4. This, of course, is the transformation that we call glide reflection. In the tessellation, it causes the change in orientation between adjacent rows of dogs. Can you read the symbols?

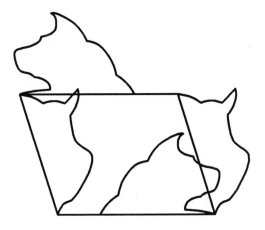

Base

1 ←——→ 3

2 ↕ 4

2

1   3

4

Modifying a Parallelogram by Translation and Glide Reflection

Assembly Instructions

Color the modified parallelogram on the transparency.

Commentary

Show the transparency.

The same combination of procedures as before was used to create this tessellating goldfish. We started with the idea of creating a fish and modified the parallelogram until its contour resembled a fish shape.

The tessellation has translational symmetry and glide-reflection symmetry, but no reflective symmetry, like the Escher tessellation that inspired it.

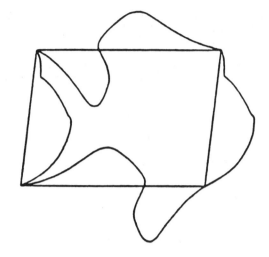

Transparency 69

"Study of Regular Division of the Plane with Human Figures"

Assembly Instructions

Use black-on-clear or colored-on-clear film.

Commentary

Show the transparency.

> *Although we have focused our discussion on designs based on a single tessellating shape, let's take a look at the tessellation that Escher prepared for use in his lithograph "Encounter."*

> *The pattern is built up from two figures, an optimist (light) and a pessimist (dark), each occurring in two different orientations. If, however, we regard the tessellating shape as a unit containing two figures, an optimist and the pessimist directly below, we find that the tessellation has precisely the same properties as Escher's tessellation of dogs.*

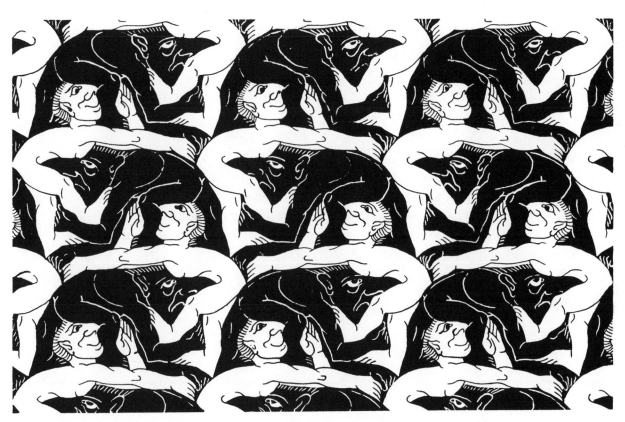

Symmetry Drawing E 63 ©1944 M. C. Escher Heirs / Cordon Art–Baarn–Holland

Transparency 70

"Encounter" Tessellating Shape

Assembly Instructions

Color the modified parallelogram on the transparency base.

Commentary

Show the transparency base with the LH overlay in place.

The tessellating shape is once again a parallelogram modified by translation and glide reflection.

Remove the LH overlay, then add the RH overlay.

Escher simply subdivided the tessellating shape into the optimist and pessimist figures, each recognizable by its contour. In general, we can subdivide any tessellating shape into as many figures as suits our fancy.

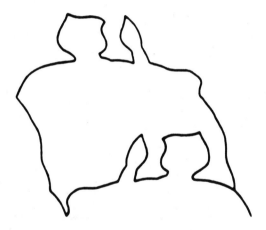

Transparency 71

Base

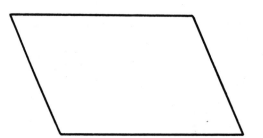

"Study of Regular Division of the Plane with Birds"

Assembly Instructions

Make two copies of the transparency base using a photocopy method. To guarantee alignment, use the same photocopy method for the overlay.

Commentary

Show the transparency base.

> *This Escher tessellation, which he used in his wood engraving "Swans," also has glide-reflection symmetry without reflection symmetry—in addition to the usual translational symmetry. Ignoring color changes, a swan can be made to exchange places with the swan just below it by first reflecting it about an appropriate vertical line, and then translating it vertically.*

Use the second copy of the tessellation to confirm this observation. Although you will have to lift the copy to effect the flip, the result will be less confusing than with the tessellation of dogs due to the coloring of the various rows.

> *To determine the underlying polygonal grid, we shall again circumnavigate a single swan, looking for points at which **more than two** tessellating shapes meet. Four swans meet at the top of each swan's head—a point that also marks the lower tip of either the left or right wing or the crest of the winding neck of adjacent swans.*

Circumnavigate a typical swan two or three times with your pointer, calling attention to the above points en route.

> *On the same swan, these points mark the vertices of a kite-shaped quadrilateral (two pairs of congruent sides of different lengths and one pair of equal angles).*

Add the overlay.

> *The basis of the tessellation is a grid of kites. Each swan fits in its parent kite in the same way as its fellow swans.*

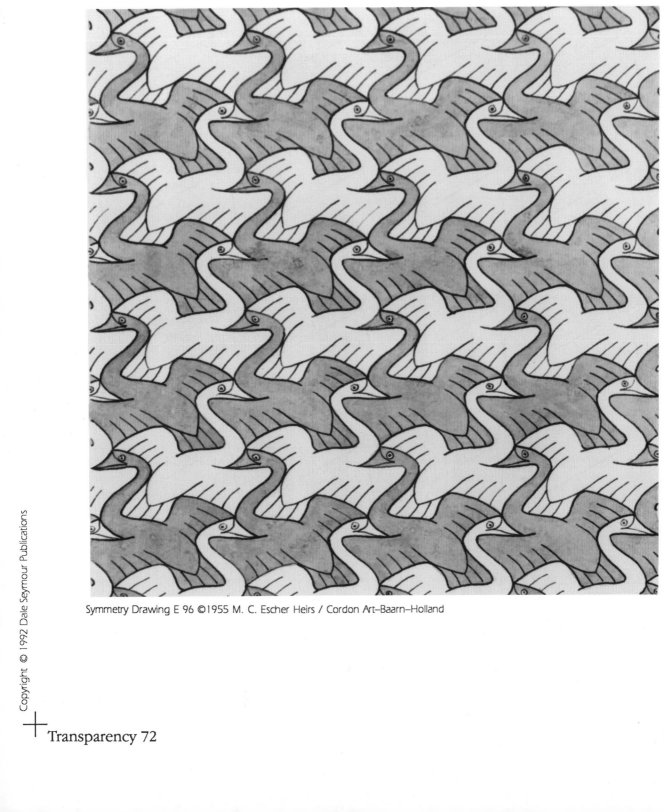

Symmetry Drawing E 96 ©1955 M. C. Escher Heirs / Cordon Art–Baarn–Holland

Base

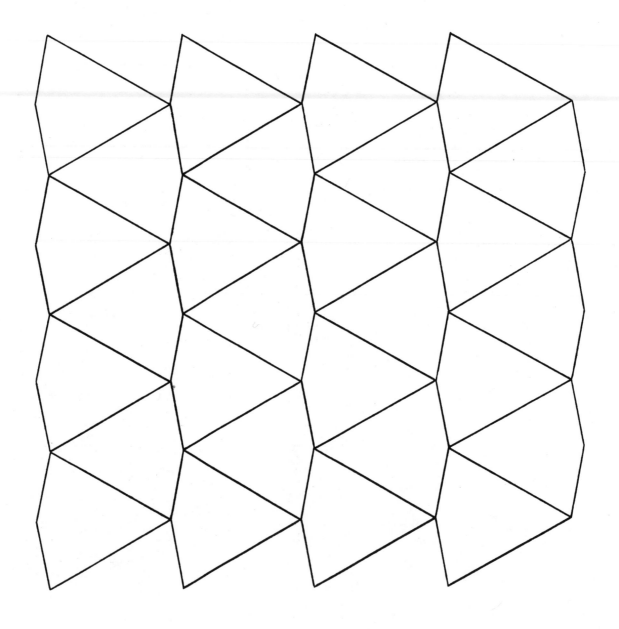

Overlay

"Swans" Tessellating Shape

Assembly Instructions

Process the piece of overlay.

   Color the figure on the transparency base and on the piece of overlay with the same color.

Commentary

Show the transparency base with overlay 1 in place.

> *Let's study the contour of a single swan inscribed in its kite-shaped quadrilateral.*

Add overlay 2.

> *Once again, we'll number the sides of the polygon for reference.*

Use the piece of overlay to demonstrate the following glide reflections as per the commentary. Following each flip, take care to reposition the piece of overlay so the subsequent vertical translation will result in coincidence of the modifications.

> *First, a modification to side 1 has been reflected in an appropriate vertical line, and the reflected modification has been translated vertically to side 2. Once again, this is the transformation that we call glide reflection. In the same way, a modification to side 3 has been glide reflected in an appropriate vertical line to side 4.*

You might mention that each vertical line of reflection in the above transformations passes through the midpoints of the pair of sides being modified.

> *Can you read the symbols?*

Remove the overlays, and demonstrate the transformations without the obscuring underlying polygon in place.

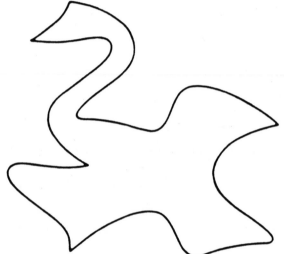

Base

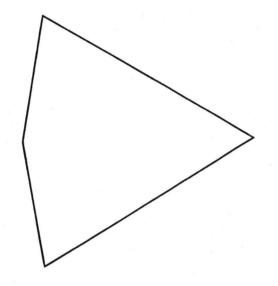

Transparency 73

Overlay 1

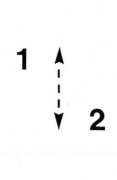

1 ↑
$\vdots$
↓ **2**

3 ↑
$\vdots$
↓ **4**

2

3

1

4

"Study of Regular Division of the Plane with Horsemen"

Assembly Instructions

Process the piece of overlay for Transparency 75.
    Process Transparency 74 using a photocopy method.
    Color the figure on the base of Transparency 75 and on its piece of overlay with the same color.

Commentary

Show Transparency 74.

> *The same modifying procedure as before—modifying two pairs of sides of a kite-shaped quadrilateral by glide reflection—can be used to create the tessellating shape for Escher's famous tessellation of horsemen.*

Show transparency 75 with the overlay in place.

> *Of all of his tessellating shapes, the creation of the horseman's contour best illustrates Escher's cunning ingenuity.*

After allowing the students sufficient time to study the horseman in its parent kite-shaped quadrilateral, remove the overlay. Use the piece of overlay on the transparency base to demonstrate the glide reflections without the obscuring underlying polygon in place.

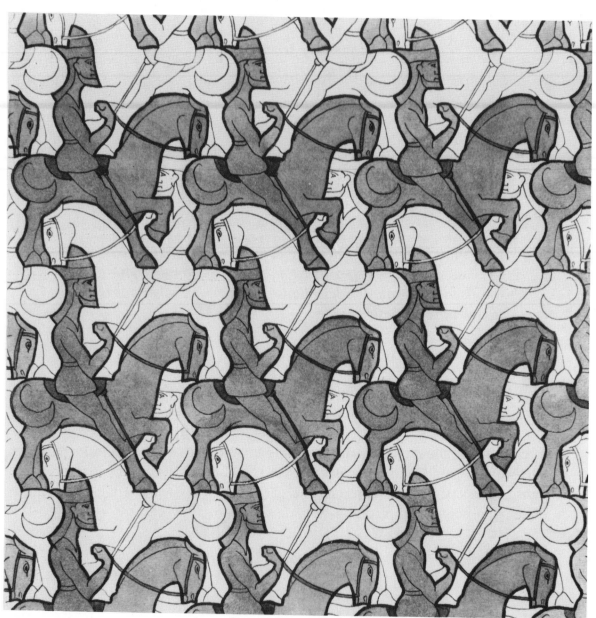

Symmetry Drawing E 67 ©1946 M. C. Escher Heirs / Cordon Art–Baarn–Holland

Transparency 74

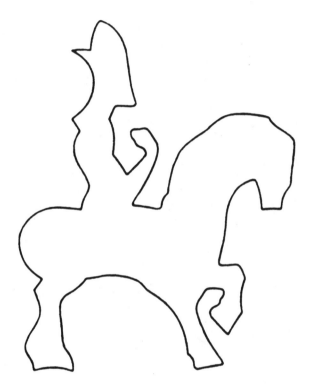

Transparency 75

Base

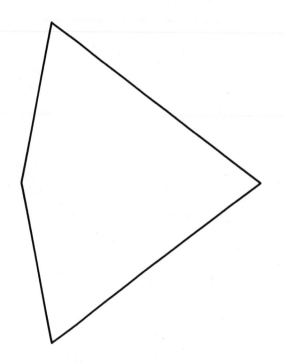

Overlay

Modifying Quadrilaterals by Glide Reflection

Assembly Instructions

Color the modified quadrilateral on each transparency.

Commentary

Show Transparency 76.

Following the same pattern of transformations as before—modifying two pairs of sides by glide reflection—we can create our own tessellating shape from a kite-shaped quadrilateral.

We started with the intent of creating a dog and modified the sides of the quadrilateral through glide reflection until it looked something like a dog. Like the Escher swan and horseman designs, the tessellation of this dog has translational symmetry and glide reflection symmetry, but no reflective symmetry.

Show Transparency 77.

The same approach was used to create this tessellating seal. The tessellating kite-shaped quadrilateral is concave (inward bending) rather than convex (outward bending). The student artist worked with no particular shape in mind, adding details to interpret the figure after the fact.

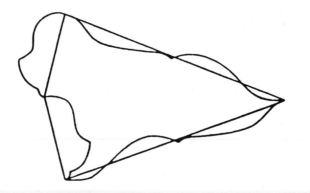

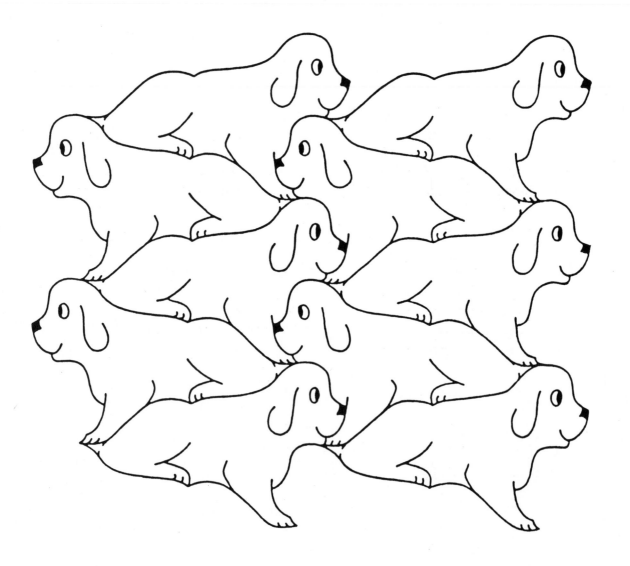

Transparency 76

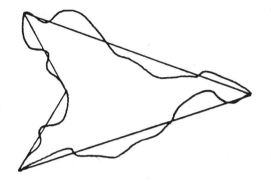

Transparency 77

Kite-Shaped Quadrilateral

Commentary

Show the transparency.

Any convex kite-shaped quadrilateral can be subdivided into two isosceles triangle by adding a vertical diagonal. When such a quadrilateral was modified to create Escher's swan, the isosceles triangle on the left was modified by glide reflection, as was the isosceles triangle on the right. This would suggest that we might be able to use glide reflection on a tessellating grid of isosceles triangles.

But a triangle has three sides. If we modify the legs of an isosceles triangle by glide reflection, how do we deal with the third side? We have two choices: reflect the modified triangle about the third side, or rotate it about the midpoint of the third side.

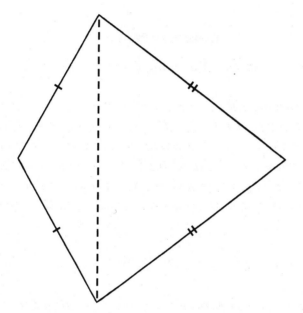

Modifying by Glide Reflection and Rotation about the Midpoint of a Side

Assembly Instructions

Color the figure on the base of Transparency 79.

For Transparency 80, use black-on-clear film or black-on-colored film whose background is the same color as on Transparency 79. Note that Transparency 80 has a horizontal format.

Commentary

Show Transparency 79 with its LH overlay in place.

For this tessellating shape, the isosceles triangle was equilateral. We modified sides 1 and 2 by glide reflection, using a sequence of steps identical to that used to create Escher's swan and horseman. Then we modified half of side 3 and rotated this change 180° about the midpoint of that side. The resulting contour resembles a bird even without the addition of interior details, but . . .

Remove the LH overlay, then add the RH overlay.

. . . once those details are added, the interpretation is reinforced.

Show Transparency 80.

Our bird tessellates in a design with translational symmetry, glide-reflection symmetry, and 2-fold rotational symmetry.

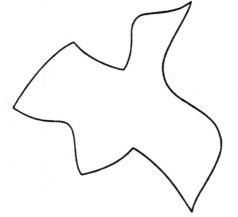

1
2

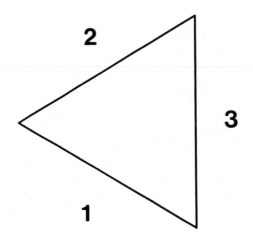

Transparency 80

Student Tessellation
(Isosceles Triangle)

.

Assembly Instructions

Color the modified triangle on the transparency.

Commentary

Show the transparency.

The triangle in this example is isosceles, but not equilateral. Rotated counterclockwise 90°, the modified triangle could be interpreted as a glamorous lady pig.

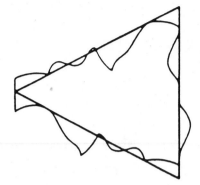

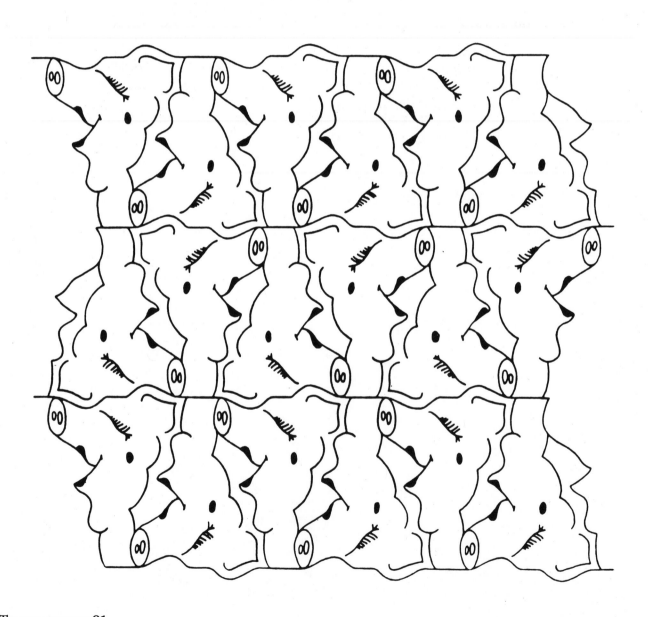

Transparency 81

Tessellations by George Escher

Commentary

When you try to create your own non-polygonal tessellating shape, you may have some specific object in mind and can try to modify some polygon (with one or more applicable procedures) until its contour resembles that object. You may also modify a polygon with random curves (and one or more applicable procedures) and interpret the resulting shape by adding interior details.

Working towards a workable contour requires patience, but the effort will make you appreciate the challenge.

As Escher's son George advises:

"Do not confuse the creation of a meaningful contour with the highlighting of the interior of a tile. These are fundamentally different things. Almost anyone can take a random shape and draw something lifelike inside its outline.

*"But it is an entirely different story to push a recalcitrant outline into a pattern that suggests, **without highlighting**, some living thing. Highlighting may be necessary to clarify a decision: is it a bird or a fish? But it is often not even necessary, if the contour is characteristic enough.*

"This discussion is not new. It is a repeat of a homily given to me by my father when I was around twelve years old . . ."

Show the transparency.

". . . and had made some tessellations like these. 'Look, it is not that difficult,' I told him. 'Why do you work so hard on such a simple task?' I soon found out."

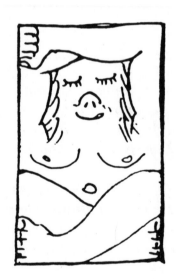

George Escher

Trim the rectangle on its RHS to the line of symmetry of the clown face

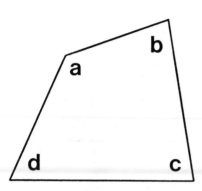

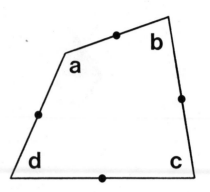

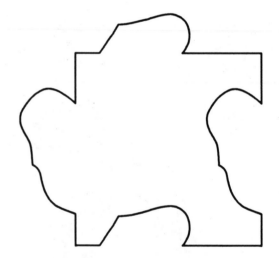

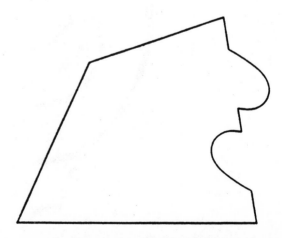

Pieces of overlay: Transparencies 36, 38, 44, 51

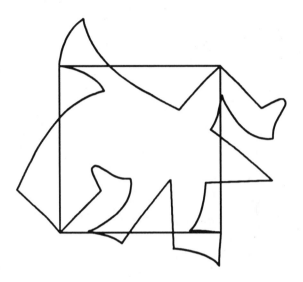

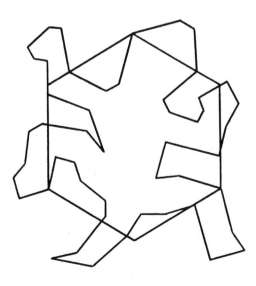

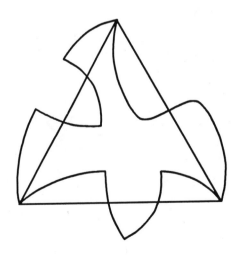

Pieces of overlay: Transparencies 68, 73, 75

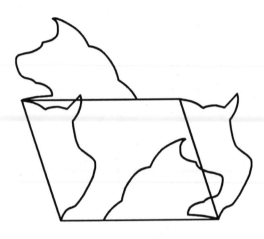

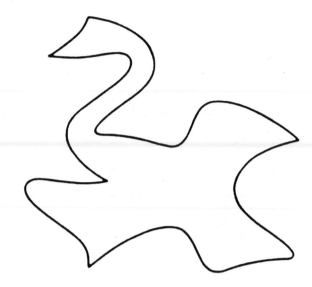

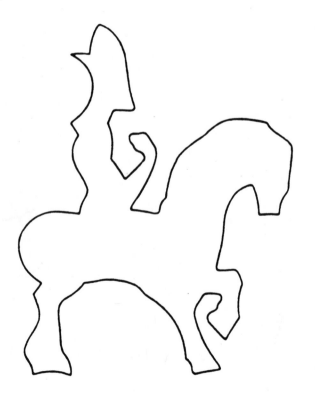

Part Three

Workshop Activities

Activities for teaching tessellating art range from the rudimentary (requiring only a sheet of graph or dot paper and a sharpened pencil) to the elaborate (requiring a computer and an expensive graphics package). In Part Three we will explore some traditional activities and introduce several innovative ones—such as fabricating a "pop-up" sponge jigsaw puzzle and printing a tessellation with a homemade rubber stamp.

Preliminary Explorations with Graph Paper

Even very young children, whatever their background, should be familiar with square floor and wall tiles—although a few ceramic "floor samples" might be displayed to introduce the topic.

In this exercise, the student will discover the consequences of modifying two adjacent sides of a square tile and be introduced to the concept of area preservation. The activity requires no introduction and should precede a formal introduction to transformations and tessellations.

Materials
Activity Sheets 1 and 2 (one per student)
sharpened pencil
ruler (optional)
2 crayons or felt-tip markers of contrasting colors

Steps
1. Copy the modification of the top of the square in the upper left-hand corner of Activity Sheet 1 to the top of each of the other squares (see Figure 1).

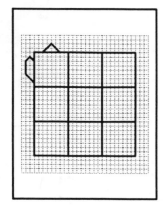 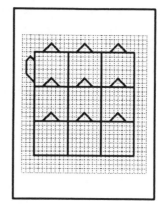

Figure 1

2. Copy the modification of the left-hand side to the left-hand sides of each of the other squares (see Figure 2).

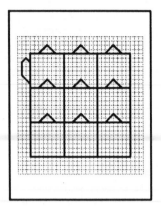
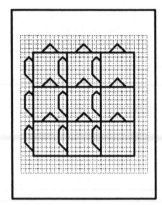

Figure 2

3. Observe that a "bump" on the top of a square is compensated for by an identical "hole" on its bottom, just as a bump on its left-hand side is compensated for by an identical hole on its right-hand side. Color a typical modified square (see Figure 3).
4. This modified square has the same area as the original or parent square. It could be used to tile, or tessellate, a floor or a wall just as a square is traditionally used. Using Activity Sheet 2, draw the tessellation of modified squares (see Figure 4).
5. Color the tessellation so adjacent or neighboring tiles that share more than one point are of different colors. This should require only two colors (see Figure 5).

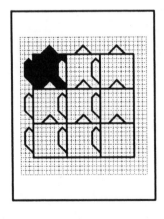
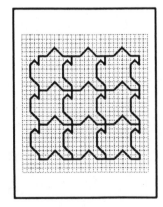
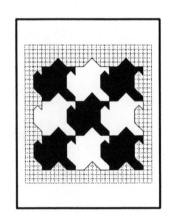

Figure 3 *Figure 4* *Figure 5*

Variations and Further Explorations

- Have the students select their own modifications, say holes rather than bumps, or a combination of bumps and holes. Stress that the initial modifications are being made to a pair of *adjacent* sides of the square.
- Explore the extension of these concepts to a tessellation of rectangles (other than a square) or a tessellation of parallelograms (other than a rectangle).
- With advanced students, you might consider the modification of three adjacent sides of a regular hexagon or a hexagon with three sets of equal and parallel sides. This will require three colors if neighboring tiles are to have different colors.
- We recommend that you confine your explorations with graph paper to the exercises suggested herein. Our objective is to introduce the tiling concept and the principle of area preservation, not to introduce transformations. Transformations are motions and should be presented as such. In the exercises that follow, there will be ample opportunity for students to stretch their imagination without the rigid structure of a grid to diminish understanding or impede progress.
- Commercial quadrille graph paper can be used in place of Activity Sheet 2.

In the remainder of Part Three, we will assume the student is familiar with transformations and simple polygonal tessellations.

Tessellating with a Template

Transformations are motions. We require methods that will compel the student to perform these motions whenever he or she draws a non-polygonal tessellation. In this section, we will explore

- how to use scissors and tape to transform a cardboard polygon into a non-polygonal tessellating shape
- how to use imagination to give a meaning to a shape
- how to draw a tessellation with a cardboard template
- how to add interpreting features to a tessellation

Exercise 1: Making a Template

Materials

2-inch square cut from coated cardboard (as from a file folder)
Activity Sheet 3 (one per student)
sharpened pencil
scissors
transparent tape

Steps

1. Draw an unsymmetrical and distinct hole on each of two adjacent sides of the cardboard square (see Figure 6). (To facilitate the eventual drawing of the tessellation, don't envelop corners!)

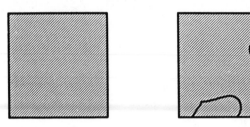

Figure 6

2. Cut out each of the holes, keeping all pieces (see Figure 7).

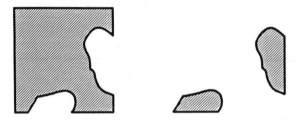

Figure 7

3. Superimpose the residual square precisely on top of any of the squares on Activity Sheet 3. Slide the residual square up (or down, if appropriate) until the edge with the hole coincides with the opposite side of the selected square. Draw tightly around the hole to obtain a congruent bump (see Figure 8).

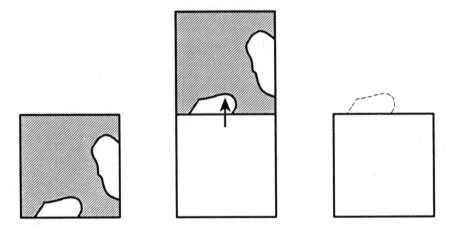

Figure 8

4. Repeat step (3), sliding the residual square to the left (or to the right) of the same square. Draw the hole as a congruent bump (see Figure 9).

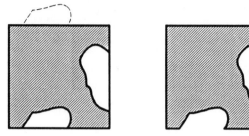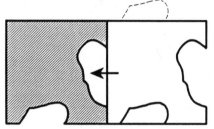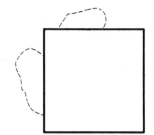

Figure 9

5. Superimpose the residual square on top of the selected square, then superimpose each of the cutouts on top of the corresponding bump. Tape each cutout to the edge of the residual square (see Figure 10).

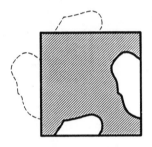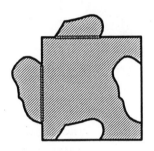

Figure 10

This non-polygonal shape will tile the plane in a tessellation with horizontal and vertical translational symmetry.

Variations and Further Explorations
■ Vary the modifying rules, using appropriate rules as set forth in Part Two.

For *rotation about the midpoint of a side,* remove a hole from one half of a side of the cardboard square. To locate the corresponding bump, rotate the residual square about the midpoint of the same side of the square on the activity sheet (see Figure 11).

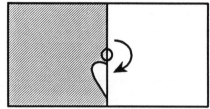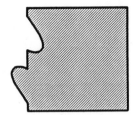

Figure 11

For *rotation about a vertex,* remove a hole from a side of the cardboard square. To locate the corresponding bump, rotate the residual square about the appropriate vertex of the square on the activity sheet to an adjacent side (see Figure 12).

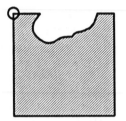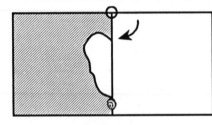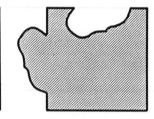

Figure 12

For *glide reflection,* remove a hole from a side of the cardboard square. To locate the corresponding bump, flip the residual square over before superimposing it on the square on the activity sheet. Slide the residual square to the side of the square on the activity sheet directly opposite the hole (see Figure 13).

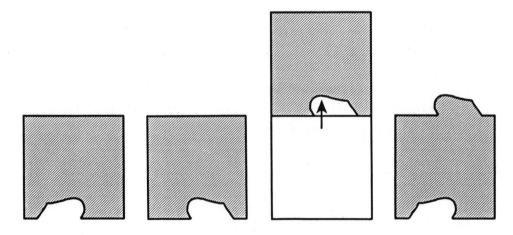

Figure 13

- Ambitious students may wish to attempt modifications involving a combination of bumps and holes per side. If they treat the modifications one bump at a time and exercise some restraint, the method is manageable (see Figure 14).
- Vary the polygon as well as, or instead of, the modifying rules. For example, the equilateral triangle at the right has been modified by rotating a hole on side 1 about vertex A to side 2, then a hole on side 2 about vertex A to side 1, and ultimately a hole on half of side 3 about its midpoint to the other half of side 3.

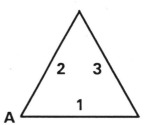

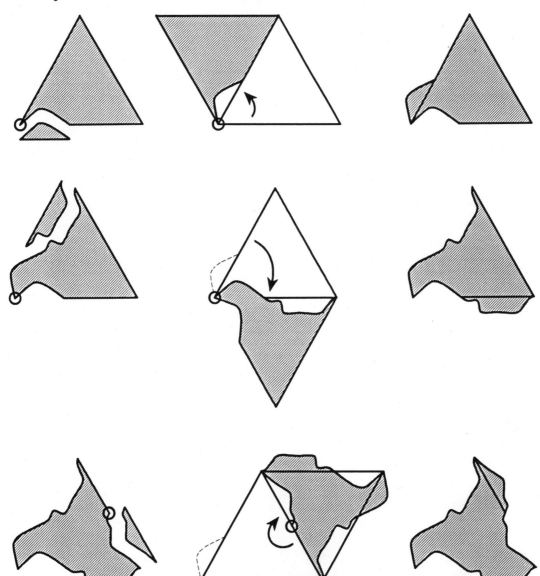

Figure 14

- For the primary student: Use at least a two-inch square imprinted with a two-thirds-inch grid. Cut out holes that intersect at least one of the grid lines subdividing a side. To position the bumps for translation, slide each cutout to the opposite side of the residual square, match the grid line(s), and tape the straight edges together (see Figure 15).

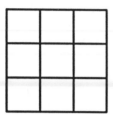

Figure 15

Exercise 2: Interpreting a Non-Polygonal Shape

Materials
tessellating template (see Exercise 1)
sharpened pencil

Steps
1. Rotate the template until the ambiguous blob reminds you of an object. You might place the template on an overhead projector and study its projected image. Use your imagination—or ask a friend for suggestions!
2. Add interior marks to the template to aid the interpretation (see Figure 16). Additional examples are presented on Activity Sheets 4 and 5.

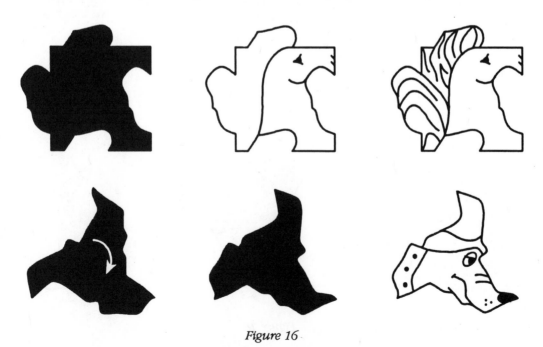

Figure 16

Exercise 3: Drawing a Tessellation with a Template

Materials

tessellating template (see Exercises 1 and 2)
sheet of carbon paper
ballpoint pen (preferably lacking an ink supply)
sharpened pencil
large sheet of drawing paper (at least 11" × 17")

Steps

1. Lay the template on the carbon paper. Go over each interior interpreting mark with a ballpoint pen to deposit a layer of carbon on the reverse side of the cardboard. Traverse each mark several times or apply pressure to increase the carbon deposit (see Figure 17).

Figure 17

2. Position the template right side up on the drawing paper. Draw tightly around its boundary with the pencil, then traverse its interior marks with the pen. (A portion of the carbon deposit will be transferred to the drawing paper. Add a fresh deposit of carbon to the template as required.)
3. Reposition the template in an adjacent location on the drawing paper by performing an appropriate transformation. Repeat step (2) as required, excluding duplicate boundary curves if preferred, to fill the drawing paper with the tessellating shape (see Figure 18).

Variations and Further Explorations

■ Since we are drawing around the template, the result will not be precisely the same as the original. Discrepancies will accumulate and can cause problems—particularly in tessellations with rotational symmetry. If the drawing paper is imprinted with dots that mark the location of the vertices of each polygon in the parent tessellation, the dots can be used to position each tessellating shape and evenly distribute the discrepancies throughout the

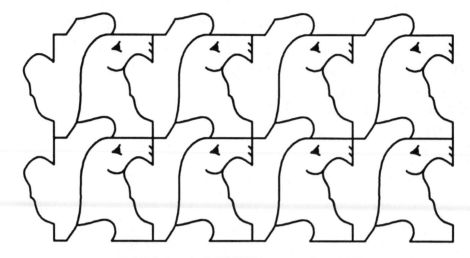

Figure 18

tessellation (see Figure 19). (If you did not envelop the corners of the polygon when removing the holes, this task will be facilitated.) Mature students should be encouraged to prepare their own dot paper with ruler and compass.

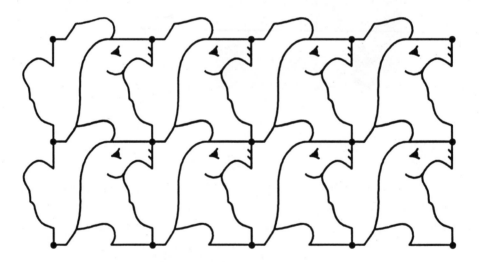

Figure 19

- To add interpreting features to a tessellation with reflection or glide-reflection symmetry, you will need two templates—each the mirror image of the other. To prepare a mirror-image template, copy the holes from the original template onto a second cardboard polygon. Prepare this template as before. Superimpose the original template precisely on top of its duplicate—carbon side up—then lay the assembly on the carbon paper. Traverse the carbon marks with the ballpoint pen, applying pressure to increase the carbon deposit on the duplicate. Add a fresh deposit of carbon to the original template. Use the appropriate template as required when drawing the tessellation.

Tessellating by Tracing

Although a simple way of creating a tessellation, the template method has its limitations. The method does not permit alteration of the parent polygon nor of a modification once it has been executed. Complex modifications consisting of a succession of bumps and holes are difficult to execute. Since we draw around the template, bumps will be slightly larger and holes slightly smaller than in the original. Elaborate interpreting marks are difficult to reproduce.

In this section, we will learn how to transform modified sides and to copy markings by tracing them in appropriate locations. The method is time consuming but can lead to impressive results.

Exercise 1: Transforming a Modified Side by Tracing

Materials
sheet of tracing paper or onionskin
Activity Sheet 6 (one per student)
ruler
sharpened pencil

Steps

1. **Translation.** Superimpose the tracing paper on the upper left-hand section of Activity Sheet 6. Trace the square and modifying curve. To translate the modifying curve to the opposite side of the upper or "target" square, slide the tracing paper until the endpoints of the modifying curve on the lower or "source" square coincide with the opposite vertices of the target square directly above. Trace the modifying curve in its new location (see Figure 20).

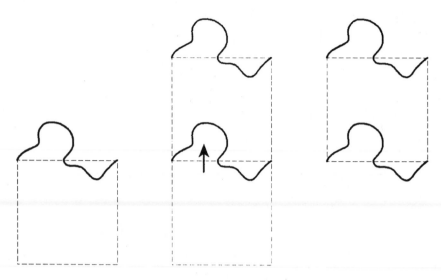

Figure 20

2. **Rotation about the Midpoint of a Side.** Superimpose the sheet of tracing paper on the upper right-hand section of Activity Sheet 6. Trace the triangle and modifying curve. To rotate the modifying curve about the midpoint of the modified side of the target triangle, turn the tracing paper 180° about the midpoint of that side until the endpoints of the modifying curve on the source triangle coincide with the endpoints of the other half side of the target triangle directly above. Trace the modifying curve in its new location. Return the tracing paper to its original orientation (see Figure 21).

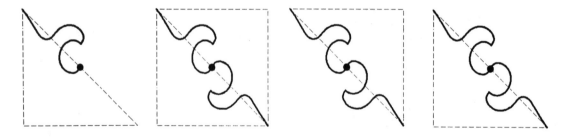

Figure 21

3. **Rotation about a Vertex.** Superimpose the sheet of tracing paper on the lower left-hand section of Activity Sheet 6. Trace the square and modifying curve. To rotate the modifying curve about the left-hand endpoint of the modified side of the target square, turn the tracing paper counterclockwise about that vertex until the endpoints of the modifying curve on the source square coincide with the endpoints of the adjacent side of the target square directly above. (To rotate about the right-hand endpoint, turn the tracing paper clockwise. For a parent square, the angle of rotation will always be

90°. Other polygons will involve angles of 60°, 90°, or 120°.) Trace the modifying curve in its new location. Return the tracing paper to its original orientation (see Figure 22).

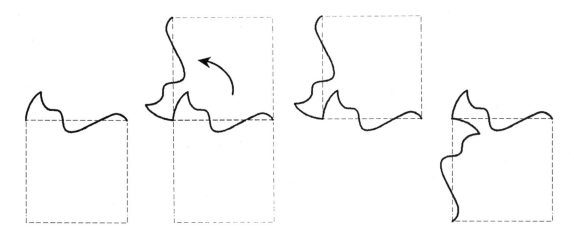

Figure 22

4. **Glide Reflection.** Superimpose the sheet of tracing paper on the lower right-hand section of Activity Sheet 6. Trace the parallelogram and modifying curve. To glide reflect the modifying curve to the opposite side of the target parallelogram, flip the tracing paper over, then slide it until the endpoints of the modifying curve on the source parallelogram coincide with the opposite vertices of the target parallelogram directly above. Trace the modifying curve, flip the tracing paper over, and trace the transformed tracing of the modifying curve in its new location (see Figure 23).

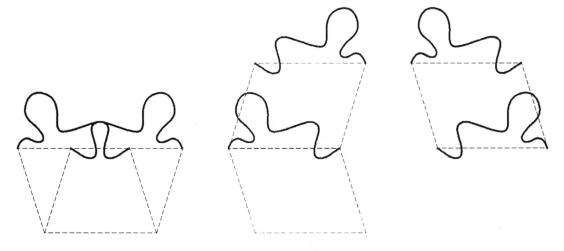

Figure 23

Variations and Further Explorations

- Use tracing paper for both source and target. When transforming a modifying curve by glide reflection, flip the lower sheet of tracing paper over, rather than the upper, and directly trace the transformed curve in its new location.

- Use an ordinary sheet of paper for both source and target with the assistance of a light box. (Markings on the lower sheet of paper will be visible through the translucent upper sheet as the unit transmits light from the intense light source.) As above, when transforming a modifying curve by glide reflection, flip the lower sheet of paper over and directly trace the transformed curve in its new location.

- You can easily improvise an inexpensive light table by straddling a plane of thick glass across two identical packing boxes or piles of heavy books with an illuminated table lamp on the floor between them. Or, use the vertical surface of a window pane in direct sunlight with masking tape to maintain the two sheets of paper in position.

Designing an original tessellating shape by tracing is a time consuming but satisfying exercise. Any tessellating polygon can serve as a basis for the shape—along with an accompanying set of appropriate modifying rules. You might have some specific object in mind and modify the polygon until its contour resembles that object, or you might modify the polygon with random curves and interpret the resulting shape by adding interior details. Working towards a decent contour requires tenacity but the effort will make you better appreciate the challenge.

A scalene quadrilateral will allow you the greatest freedom and flexibility when you attempt your first design. As you make your preliminary sketches, you may find that you want to alter the shape of your original polygon—and with a scalene quadrilateral, you can. However long its sides and whatever the size of its angles, a quadrilateral will tessellate the plane if each of its sides is rotated 180° about its midpoint. In the exercise that follows, we will use such a quadrilateral for illustrative purposes. The steps are universally applicable.

Exercise 2: Modifying a Polygon by Tracing

Materials
tracing paper or onionskin
ruler
sharpened pencil
masking tape

Steps

1. Draw a tessellating polygon on a sheet of tracing paper. Tape this fixed source polygon to your drawing surface.
2. Trace the source polygon onto a second sheet of tracing paper. This movable polygon will serve as your target until such time as it may replace the source polygon.
3. Modify appropriate half sides or sides of the source polygon with curves.
4. Trace each modifying curve in the identical location on the target polygon, then trace the transformed curve in its appropriate new location (see Figure 24).

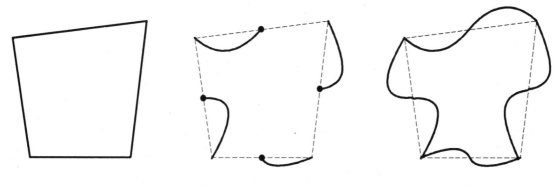

Figure 24

5. Study the contour of the resulting tessellating shape. Make changes or refinements in your modifying curves and parent polygon (if applicable) until the shape resembles some object. Add interior details to strengthen that interpretation. Replace the source polygon by the target polygon if beneficial, then proceed with a fresh target polygon. Refine the drawing through as many successive tracings as necessary (see Figure 25).

Figure 25

Variations and Further Explorations

- When using glide reflection, flip over the source polygon, rather than the target, and trace the transformed modifying curve directly in its new location on the target polygon.

- Coloring books are an excellent resource for the addition of interior interpreting features such as eyes, noses, and mouths to shapes resembling animals. A drawing may even suggest a potential contour (see Figure 26).

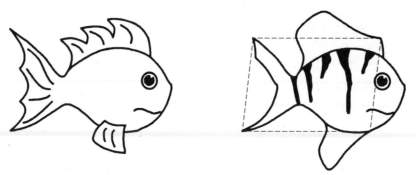

Figure 26. The fish (left) inspired the tessellating goldfish (right).

- Any tessellating shape designed by tracing can be turned into a durable template by gluing a copy of it to a piece of laminated card stock, then cutting the shape out. If rubber cement is used, the paper pattern can be detached easily.
- Refer to the notes at the end of Exercise 1 that deal with the improvisation and use of an inexpensive light table.

Exercise 3: Drawing a Tessellation by Tracing

Materials

tessellating shape (see Exercise 2)
light table
masking tape
large sheet of translucent drawing paper
ruler
sharpened pencil or black ink fineliner

Steps

1. Tape the paper with the tessellating shape to the light table. If the modifying rules involve reflection or glide reflection, prepare a tracing of the mirror image of the shape and any interior marks. Tape it alongside the original, then use where appropriate.
2. To avoid the problem of grid lines in your finished design, draw the *mirror image* of the underlying polygonal grid on the *back* of the drawing paper.
3. Lay the drawing paper face up on top of the tessellating shape or pattern on the light table. Align a polygon in the grid with the parent polygon. Trace all modifying curves and marks with pencil or ink. Move the drawing paper until an adjacent polygon and some portion of its modified boundary aligns precisely with the pattern (or its mirror image). Trace all new curves and marks. Repeat as required (see Figure 27).

 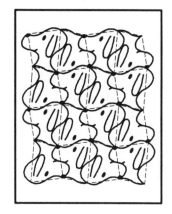 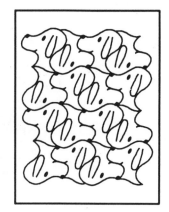

Figure 27

Variations and Further Explorations

- Turn the tessellating shape into a template and create the art as in the preceding section.
- Ink gives a better contrast than pencil, but errors are harder to repair. If you use pencil, you can improve the contrast by photocopying your drawing, processing it through a thermal transparency maker, and photocopying the resulting acetate.

Creating a Tessellating Collage

In this section, we will explore unique and attractive ways of presenting your tessellation.

Exercise 1: Assembling a Construction Paper Collage

Materials
tessellating template
construction paper (at least two contrasting colors)
sharpened pencil
felt-tip marker
scissors
large sheet of poster board
glue

Steps
1. Draw around the template several times on each sheet of construction paper. If appropriate, transfer interior marks and intensify them with the marker.
2. Cut out the tessellating shapes.
3. Glue the tessellating shapes to the poster board so adjacent shapes that share more than one point are of a different color (see Figure 28).

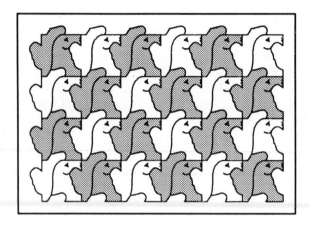

Figure 28

Variations and Further Explorations

■ Mark the location of the vertices of each polygon in the parent tessellation on the poster board. Use these dots to position the shapes and to evenly distribute discrepancies throughout the collage.

■ Cut the tessellating shapes out of contrasting colors of foil wrap or lively gift wrap.

Exercise 2: Making a Felt Wall Hanging

Materials

tessellating template based on a 2-inch square
sheet of plain paper
sharpened pencil
felt or self-adhesive felt (9" × 12") (one source of self-adhesive felt is Ellison Educational Equipment Inc., P.O. Box 8209, Newport Beach, CA 92658)
pins
scissors
felt of a contrasting color (14" × 25")
2 wooden dowels (½" × 16")
fabric glue
chalk fabric pencil

Steps

1. Draw tightly around the template on the paper to produce nine identical patterns.
2. Pin each pattern to the 9-by-12-inch piece of felt. Cut out the shapes.
3. Make a 1¼-inch hem on each narrow end of the 14-by-25-inch piece of felt. Attach the long free edge of the hem to the back of the wall hanging with a thin line of fabric glue. Slip a dowel into each sleeve to protrude 1 inch at each opening.

4. On the front of the wall hanging, mark a grid of dots spaced 2 inches apart in a diamond pattern (see below) with the chalk pencil.
5. Glue the felt shapes to the wall hanging by matching appropriate vertices of the parent square with the dots (see Figure 29).

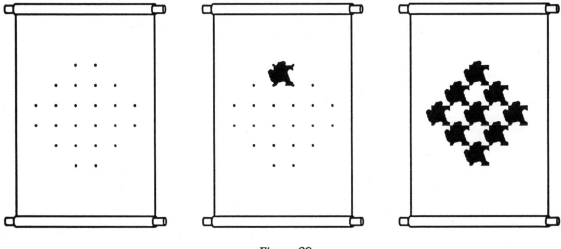

Figure 29

Activities with Pop-Up Sponge

Classic jigsaw puzzles have interlocking pieces of different shapes that fit together in only one way. A tessellating shape could form the basis of a jigsaw puzzle of only one shape in which the pieces would fit together in a multitude of ways.

Turning a tessellating shape into a jigsaw puzzle is a more difficult problem than you might initially perceive. A disassembled jigsaw puzzle of different shapes will fit back together exclusively in the way in which it was cut—however crudely that might be! If rigid, the interlocking pieces in a tessellating jigsaw puzzle must be cut with extreme precision so they can be exchanged or oriented differently, yet still fit together. Alternatively, the pieces must be cut from a material with enough flexibility that minor imperfections will be inconsequential. The material should be easy to cut with scissors, yet thick enough so the interlocking pieces can be handled by a child. Fortunately, there is a material that meets all these specifications: compressed, or pop-up, sponge.

Pop-up sponge is available in 8½-by-12-inch (or larger) sheets in a variety of pastel colors. When purchased, it has the appearance and thickness of felt and can be drawn on and cut like cardboard. When immersed in water, the material expands ("pops") to approximately a ½-inch thickness—a fascinating experience on its own! Incidentally, the dry material will swell when exposed to any source of moisture, including humid air, and will not return to its original thickness as it dehydrates. It should be kept in the reclosable plastic bag in which it is packaged until ready to use.

Exercise 1: Making a Pop-Up Sponge Jigsaw Puzzle

Materials

sheet of 8½" × 12" pop-up sponge (available from Dale Seymour Publications; see page 279)
tessellating template
sharpened pencil
waterproof medium felt-tip marker
scissors
pail of water

Steps

1. Position the template anywhere on the sponge. Draw closely around its boundary with the pencil. If applicable, transfer interior interpreting marks.
2. Repeat step (1) as many times as you require tessellating shapes. Keep the shapes disconnected (see Figure 30). Don't attempt to economize by tessellating. This will reduce the possibility of the material tearing when you cut out the shapes in step (4).

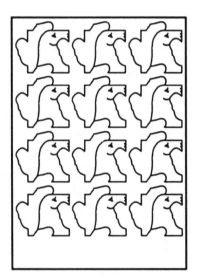

Figure 30

3. If applicable, go over interior marks with the marker. You may also dramatically define the contour of the individual shapes by traversing each boundary.
4. Cut out the shapes, cutting just inside the boundary to compensate for size variations in the bumps and holes that were introduced when we drew around the template.
5. Immerse the shapes in water (see Figure 31). When they have completely expanded, squeeze out the excess moisture.
6. Assemble your tessellating jigsaw puzzle.

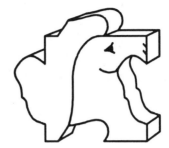

Figure 31

Variations and Further Explorations

- A well-defined contour and interior interpreting marks will help the younger child properly align the shapes when the tessellation is assembled. This is particularly useful in tessellations with reflection or glide-reflection symmetry.
- The sponge will not return to its original thickness as it dehydrates, but will shrink to about one-half of its expanded thickness. The dehydrated sponge will expand to the same thickness if immersed in water again.
- If your tessellating shape was designed by tracing, you can turn it into a template as described previously or transfer all markings with carbon paper. Position carbon paper between the traced shape and the sheet of sponge, then traverse both the boundary and interior interpreting marks with a ballpoint pen. Repeat for each shape as required. Cut along the boundary.
- Pop-up sponge is not a precision material. Individual sheets have different thicknesses and expansion capacities. Where possible, cut all shapes from the same sheet. Barring that, we recommend that you test the expansion capacity of your various sheets of sponge as follows: Number the sheets, cut a ½-inch square from a corner of each, and write the assigned number on the square with a waterproof marker. Immerse the squares in water, squeeze out the excess moisture, then compare the length, width, and height of the expanded squares.
- Cut the shapes from sponge of contrasting colors. Use sheets of compatible expansion capacity. (Test the compatibility as described above.)

Throughout his life, Maurits Escher was drawn to "rhythmic repetition." He took great pride and pleasure in his technical mastery of woodcut printing. Escher would painstakingly carve a tessellating unit into pear wood and then fill a surface with contiguous prints of it. Although we will not attempt to duplicate his efforts, in the exercises that follow we will attempt to "mirror" Escher's printing activities with simple materials. It is hoped that by performing these exercises you will gain some appreciation of the craftsmanship of the graphic artist as well as discover intriguing and practical ways of executing a tessellation from a single repeating unit.

Exercise 2: Printing a Tessellation with a Sponge Shape

Materials

large sheet of drawing paper
piece of pop-up sponge (a 3-inch square is usually adequate)
tessellating template
sharpened pencil
scissors
pail of water
tempera paint
2 paper plates

Steps

1. Imprint the drawing paper with dots that mark the location of the vertices of each polygon in the parent tessellation. Mature students could be encouraged to prepare their own dot paper with ruler and compass. (Or, omit the dots and align the shapes in step (5) by eye alone.)
2. Make a single sponge shape as described in Exercise 1. Immerse the shape in water and squeeze out the excess moisture.
3. Pour about one-fourth of a cup of paint into one of the paper plates. Distribute the material by tilting the plate from side to side. Holding the moist sponge face up and by its edges, dip it into the paint. Generously coat the entire printing surface of the sponge.
4. Transfer the coated sponge to the second paper plate. Rub it around the bottom of the plate to evenly distribute the paint on the printing surface and to allow any excess to be evenly absorbed by the sponge. The coated surface should reveal its spongy texture.
5. Still holding the sponge by its edges, align the vertices of the parent polygon over one set of dots on the drawing paper. (If you did not envelop any corners of the parent polygon when you prepared the template, this task will be facilitated.) Gently lay the painted side down, straight onto the drawing paper, vertex to corresponding dot. Pat over the entire top surface of the sponge using a light, even pressure—then lift straight up to expose the colored impression of your tessellating shape.
6. Fill the drawing paper with shapes so no printed shape shares more than one point with another (see Figure 32). (In most tessellations of modified quadrilaterals or triangles, the printed shapes will alternate.) You should be able to use a coated sponge several times before the paint will require replenishing. Don't expect precision results!
7. Allow four hours for the paint to dry.

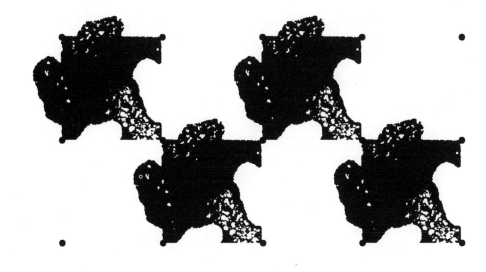

Figure 32

Variations and Further Explorations

- Tempera paint is water soluble, allowing for quick and easy cleanup with water.
- The sponge shape can be used over and over. Just rinse it with water. Always moisten the sponge before using it again.
- After the paint has dried, print in appropriate adjacent locations using a contrasting color. With some modified polygons, like hexagons, you can use a third color.
- Try printing on notebooks, book covers, blackboards, paper bags . . . just about anything!
- Sponges can be used to print on sweat shirts or T-shirts. Use a fabric paint that does not require ironing. Washing will remove any "stickiness" from the paint (see "Making a Tessellating T-Shirt").

Tessellating with a Homemade Rubber Stamp

Sponge printing is an effective but primitive technique—primitive by nature and in the quality of the print. Some degree of surface expansion is inevitable when the sponge is moistened. The wet sponge is awkward to handle and difficult to align precisely with the lattice of dots. Unless a very light pressure is applied to the sponge during printing, the thick paint tends to ooze outside the boundary. The sporadic air holes in the expanded sponge leave a mottled print that detracts from the repetitive nature of the interlocking shapes.

Relief or block printing is a practical and more precise alternative. This technique involves the use of a raised stamp, that is, a raised printing shape attached to a supporting block or mount. Classic examples of relief prints are brass rubbings and the simple potato prints you may have experimented with as a child.

The printing shape will be a tessellating one. The mount to which the tessellating shape is attached must be transparent to allow for precision alignment of the shapes during printing. We have experimented with a variety of materials from which one might cut (or carve) the printing shape, from soft cardboard to plastic foam from a delicatessen tray. The best and most reliable results were obtained with self-adhesive rubber—an inexpensive, absorbent material. To apply color, we will use an large cloth stamp pad with the usual stamp pad ink.

Exercise 1: Making a Rubber Stamp

Materials

tessellating template
sheet of plain paper
sharpened pencil
rubber cement
piece of self-adhesive rubber (available from Dale Seymour Publications; see page 279)
scissors
clear plastic stamp mount (make it yourself, or see page 279)
chalk fabric pencil
ballpoint pen

Steps

1. Draw around the template on a scrap of paper slightly larger than the tessellating shape. Glue the "pattern" to the waxy backing of a piece of self-adhesive rubber of the same size.
2. Cut *clockwise* around the boundary of the shape, keeping the shape to the *right* of the scissor blades. The pattern and waxy backing will cut precisely, but the rubber will tend to protrude beyond the boundary in the vicinity of curves. Detach the pattern to reveal the waxy backing. Trim the rubber until it is flush with the boundary of the backing (see Figure 33).

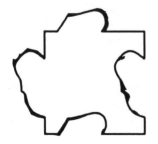 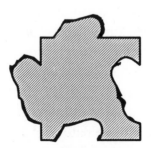 

Figure 33

3. Peel away the waxy backing from the rubber shape to expose its self-adhesive surface. Attach the shape to the uninterrupted surface of the transparent mount with one smooth motion (see Figure 34).

Figure 34

4. If appropriate, add interior interpreting features with the chalk pencil. Go over the marks with a ballpoint pen to score the surface of the rubber. Fill in solid areas (see Figure 35). Use light short repetitive strokes to reduce beading of the material.

Figure 35

Variations and Further Explorations

■ Stress that the rubber surface of the printing shape will be the mirror image of the template. Its impression will be the mirror image once again and hence the same as the template.

■ Warning! The rubber is susceptible to irreversible marring if compressed for a prolonged period of time.

■ To transfer interior features from a paper drawing, trace the mirror image of all marks on translucent paper, then align this pattern with the mounted rubber shape against a light source. Using a sharp pencil, pierce the interior marks with a succession of small dots to score the surface of the rubber.

Remove the pattern, then join the dots with appropriate scoring curves.

- Each rubber stamp can be used again and again. The mount can also be recycled. Tear off the rubber region until only traces of the adhesive remain. Be sure to dislodge the plastic film between the rubber and the adhesive. Spray WD-40® (available in most hardware stores) onto a paper towel in a well-ventilated room. Rub the adhesive remnants with the wet towel until the surface of the mount is smooth. Wash the mount with soap and water, then wipe off any residual greasy film with a dry paper towel. (Warning: Other solvents such as rubber cement thinner may cause the plastic in the mount to crack.)

- Plastic stamp mounts may be bought from Dale Seymour Publications (see page 279) or made from plastic scraps (see Figure 36). For each mount, you will require a 4-by-5½-by-⅛-inch piece of plastic and a piece 2-by-5½-by-⅛-inch (or thicker) for the handle. Attach the smaller piece by its narrow lengthwise edge to the larger piece in a T formation. Use a solvent like methylene chloride or an epoxy glue to bond the two pieces together.

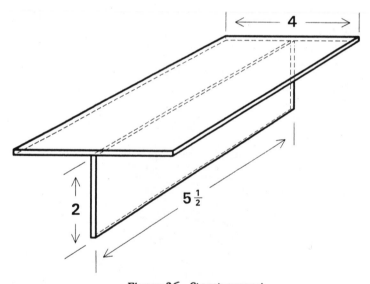

Figure 36. Stamp mount.

Exercise 2: Printing a Tessellation with a Rubber Stamp
Materials
large sheet of drawing paper
tessellating rubber stamp (see Exercise 1)
felt-tip marker
piece of thick plastic film or wax paper (6" × 9")
section of newspaper
large cloth stamp pad (4½" × 7½")
paper towels

Steps

1. Imprint the drawing paper with dots that mark the location of the vertices of each polygon in the parent tessellation. To facilitate alignment of the rubber shape during printing, use the marker to place a small dot on the back of the transparent mount directly above each vertex of the parent polygon.

2. Cut a hole slightly larger than the rubber printing shape in the center of the plastic film. Center this "shield" on the stamp pad (see Figure 37). (When the stamp is pressed into the pad, the shield will protect the surface of the mount surrounding the shape from undesirable deposits of ink.)

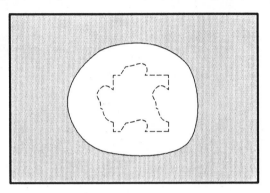

Figure 37

3. Place the drawing paper on the newspaper to promote even impressions and to provide an absorbent pad for any residual ink that may soak through the drawing paper.

4. Saturate the rubber printing shape with ink by pressing the stamp firmly into the stamp pad. The entire printing shape must contact the pad. Adjust the location of the shield as required. Wipe off any drops of ink that may inadvertently deposit around the rubber region on the mount. (The handle of the mount available from Dale Seymour Publications is centered, so pressure is applied mainly to the rubber region when an impression is made. It will not be necessary to wipe off superfluous ink deposits provided the edges of the mount have been sheilded during inking.)

5. Align the vertices of the parent polygon of the printing shape over one set of dots on the drawing paper. Gently lay the mount down, straight onto the drawing paper, vertex to corresponding dot. Apply a firm, even pressure to the top of the mount, then lift straight up to expose the colored impression of your tessellating shape.

6. Fill the drawing paper with shapes so no printed shape shares more than one point with another (see Figure 38). (In most tessellations of modified quadrilaterals or triangles, the printed shapes will alternate.) Saturate the rubber printing shape with a fresh supply of ink before each impression.

7. Allow an hour for the ink to dry.

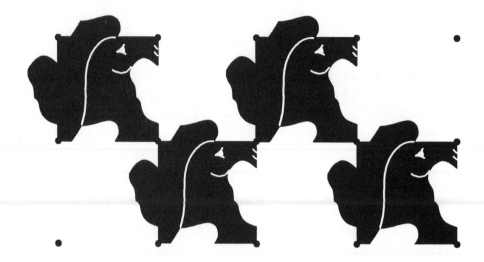

Figure 38

Variations and Further Explorations

- To print tessellations with reflection or glide-reflection symmetry, you will require two stamps—each the mirror image of the other.
- Once all regions have been printed, rinse the stamp(s) under running water. Press the residual moisture into a paper towel, then print in appropriate adjacent locations using contrasting colors. With some modified polygons, like hexagons, you can use a third color.
- Plastic from ordinary plastic shopping bags makes excellent stamp pad shields. You can further protect the paper from accidental deposits of ink by shielding all but the area to be printed with scrap paper.
- The rubber stamp can be used again and again. Rinse it with water before storing. If preferred, recycle the mount by removing all traces of the rubber region with WD-40® (see p. 246).

As a culmination to a study of tessellations, have your students print a tessellation on a T-shirt. The exercise will prove both fun and practical. Fabric paint and paint brushes can be purchased in most craft stores.

Exercise Three: Making a Tessellating T-Shirt

Materials

cotton T-shirt
section of newspaper
sheet of drawing paper
sharpened pencil
fabric paint (water-soluble, heat-setting)
tessellating rubber stamp (see Exercise 1)
medium artist's paint brush
fine artist's paint brush
paper towels

Steps

1. Wash the T-shirt. Do not use fabric softener. Iron when dry to remove wrinkles.
2. Lay out the T-shirt front side up. Line the inside with newspaper to promote even impressions and to prevent paint from soaking through the garment.
3. Imprint the drawing sheet with a grid of dots that mark the location of the vertices of each polygon in the parent tessellation. Select an appealing configuration of dots, center it horizontally on top of the T-shirt, and transfer the dots to the front of the garment by piercing the paper with the pencil. (For illustrative purposes, we will use a printing shape based on a two-inch square modified by translation and make nine impressions of it in a diamond configuration.)
4. Shake the fabric paint well. Brush a liberal amount of paint on the rubber printing shape with the medium paint brush. Spread the paint to the very border of the printing shape, keeping the layer of paint thicker in the center. Wipe off any accidental deposits of paint on the mount.
5. Align the vertices of the parent polygon of the printing shape over one set of dots on the T-shirt. Gently lay the mount down, straight onto the fabric, vertex to corresponding dot. Apply a firm, even pressure to the top of the mount, then lift straight up to expose the colored impression of your tessellating shape. Use the fine brush to work the paint into the fibers and to patch any noticeable flaws in the impression.
6. Immediately rinse the stamp under running water, then press any residual moisture into a paper towel.
7. Repeat steps (4) through (6) to fill the printing areas with shapes so no printed shape shares more than one point with another. (In most tessellations, the printed shapes will alternate.) Rinse the stamp under running water and apply fresh layer of paint before each impression.

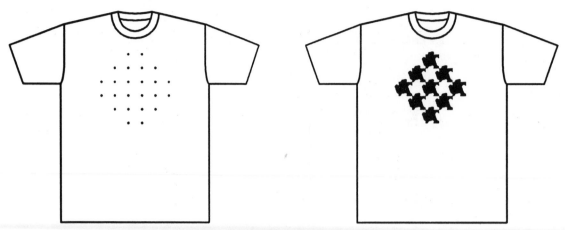

Figure 39

8. Allow the paint to dry thoroughly, preferably overnight, before heatsetting. Keep the newspaper in place as the paint dries.

9. Turn the T-shirt inside out and iron with a dry heat at a hot setting for one minute. The paint will then be permanent and the garment can be machine washed in a gentle cycle with mild soap.

Variations and Further Explorations

- To facilitate alignment of the rubber shape during printing, use a felt-tip marker to place a small dot on the back of the mount directly above each vertex of the parent polygon.

- Stiff or short-haired brushes will give you the most control. Patch flaws with discretion since overlapping layers of paint will be conspicuous with most fabric colors other than black.

- Use more than one fabric color. After heatsetting, add features to the shapes with a waterproof marker. (Indentations on the rubber shape will fill in as you make the impressions.)

- Protect the fabric from accidental deposits of paint by shielding all but the area to be printed with scrap paper. To remove any accidental deposits of paint, blot the excess, and wipe with a damp cloth while the paint is still wet.

- When finished, clean the brushes with water. Rinse the stamp several times under running water, then press any excess moisture into a dry paper towel until no traces of paint transfer to the surface of the towel.

Activity Sheet 1

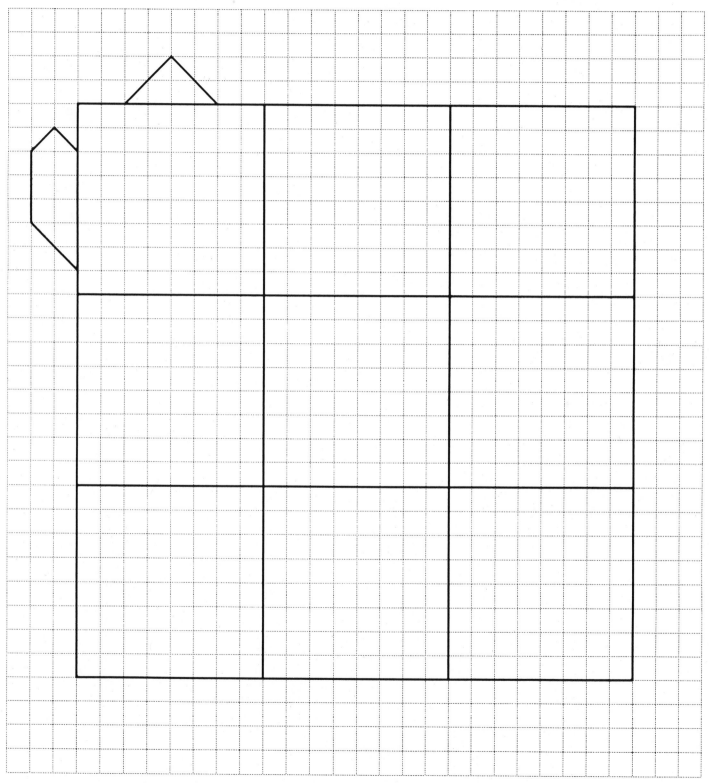

Activity Sheet 2

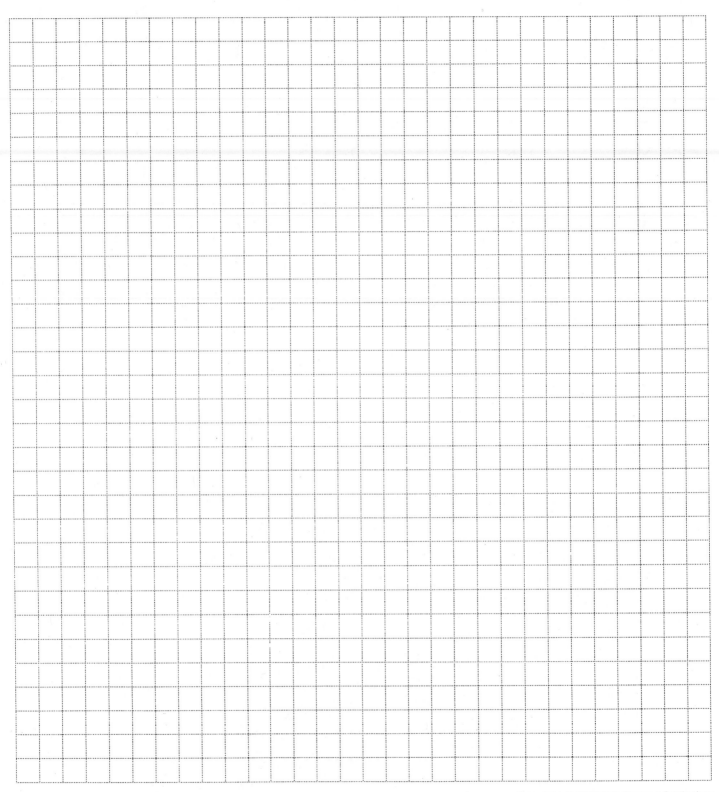

Activity Sheet 3

Activity Sheet 4

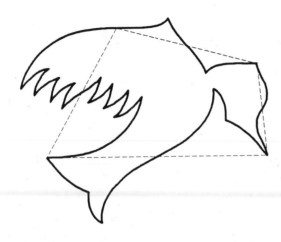

Can you make ...

a piranha?

a bird?

an angel fish?

Try one!

Activity Sheet 5

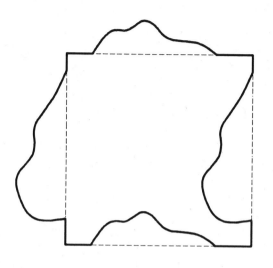

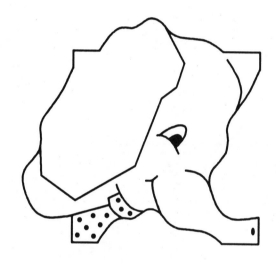

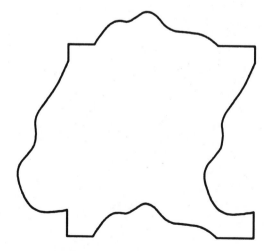

Use your imagination!

Activity Sheet 6

Translation

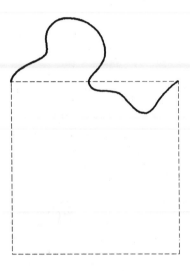

Rotation about the Midpoint of a Side

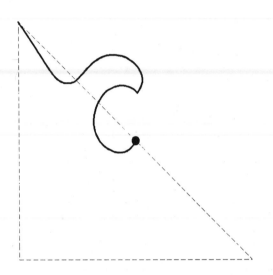

Rotation about a Vertex

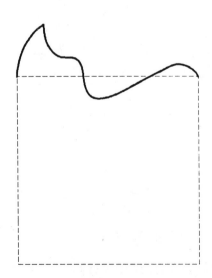

Glide Reflection

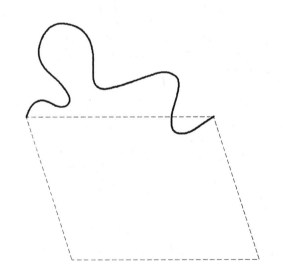

Part Four

Creating Tessellations with Computers

The proliferation of computer programs to create graphic images has followed the evolution of the microcomputer. It is impossible to cover in detail the graphic programs for the many types of computers. It would be difficult to find a microcomputer that did not have a graphic program written for it.

This section is a primer for those who have limited computer experience with graphic programs. It outlines the requirements for the production of Escher-like tessellations with a graphic program and demonstrates techniques for producing them.

Many Different Programs

Some programming languages can be used to create non-polygonal tessellations, and they should have cursor indicator and control. Languages like LOGO, with its turtle graphics, are suitable. You will find Kenney and Bezuszka's *Tessellations Using LOGO* a useful starting point.

Two types of graphic programs can easily be used for developing non-polygonal tessellations in an interactive way. They are called *paint programs* and *draw programs*.

Graphic programs manipulate images in the same way word processors manipulate words. Elements can be added or removed. They can be duplicated, moved, stretched, rotated, and even skewed in some systems. In short, all the word-processing techniques have been translated into graphic-processing techniques.

Program Control and Functions

Most graphic programs have adopted a menu control system. Usually, its presence is indicated by a menu bar across the top of the screen. Any menu item can be expanded into a submenu. One menu, usually named File, is for saving, retrieving, and printing graphic images. Another menu, usually named Edit, is for modifying or editing your graphics. Other menus, with names like Options, Misc, Pick, View, and Change, provide additional functions such as zoom, rotate, and flip.

Most graphic programs have an icon menu of graphic tools, usually on the left-hand side of the screen. Paint tools include pen and brush lines, spray patterns, and fill beaker or roller. Draw tools include several options for both straight and curved lines.

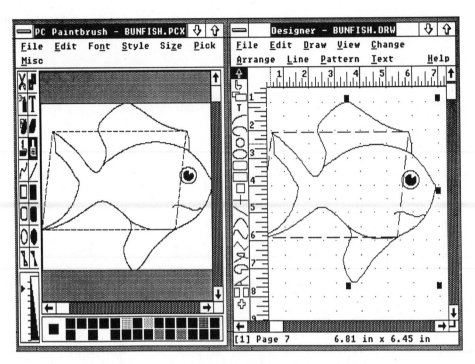

Figure 1. Menu systems of a paint (left) and draw (right) program.

Using a Mouse

Graphic programs are usually controlled by a pointing device such as a mouse. You hold down the mouse button, move it in the desired direction, and then release the button. A line or figure appears on the monitor in the process. Such a system is ideal for freehand drawing. The same procedure is used to *drag* or *move* an object in the work area. All graphic programs allow the user to draw straight and curved lines, as well as regular figures such as circles and squares, with a mouse.

Choosing or selecting a tool, menu item, or part of the artwork with a mouse occurs frequently in this text. You position the mouse cursor over the item to be selected and press the mouse button rapidly. You should have a sense of clicking the mouse button. In this text, we will describe this operation as *click*.

Paint Programs

The distinguishing feature about paint programs is that they generate a graphic image with a set of picture elements called *pixels*. Each pixel is usually seen as black on a white background. A black pixel is said to be in the "on" state. Normally, it is difficult to see an individual pixel without the benefit of magnification.

Lines are composed of a series of adjacent pixels. Lines forming closed loops can be filled; that is, all the picture elements within the loop can be on.

Many paint programs have a display enlargement feature called *zoom*, which allows easy pixel viewing and editing. In the zoom mode, pixels are indicated by large rectangles or squares, and individual pixels can easily be turned on and off. The zoom feature clearly shows the nature of lines in paint programs.

Paint programs have a lasso selection tool, which is required to do tessellations on a computer, to isolate part of a line that is to then be copied or moved. Some paint programs allow parts of an image to be selected by a closed loop drawn freehand around the desired part of the image. With this feature, irregular parts of an image can be isolated. However, some paint programs' lasso tools will select the entire area defined by a rectangular enclosure. This rectangular frame must not block out the painting area within the frame, or it will be impossible to see the line's position with respect to the other lines in the painting. Other paint programs' lasso tools will select only the line, by, for example, tracing around the figure contained in the lasso.

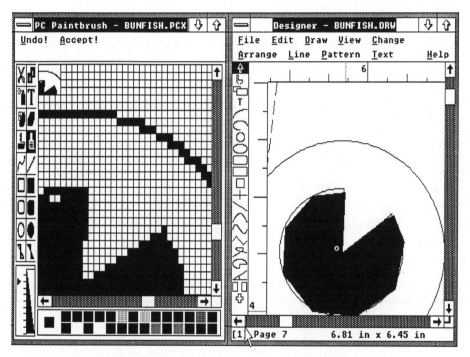

Figure 2. Paint (left) and draw (right) screens zoomed.

With paint programs, one can draw any kind of line manually and draw non-polygonal figures. Paint programs are relatively inexpensive. Some are packaged with other software packages or with hardware devices such as mouses or hand scanners.

Draw Programs

Draw programs produce images that are constructed with mathematical functions. Every line is an unique object. When you magnify a region of the line, you see only the portion of the line generated by the function. When you magnify a region of a curved line, you see an arc—not pixels. This distinction is illustrated in Figure 2.

When paint and draw images are compared in their normal view, as in Figure 1, nothing suggests that they were generated by two such radically different methods. However, when the two graphics are magnified, their differences are apparent. Notice that the enlargement on the left of Figure 2 shows the pixels. The draw program image on the right is redrawn by the function on a different scale, as the rulers indicate.

Draw programs offer precision in image construction. Straight and curved lines are generated precisely. Each line can be combined with other lines to form a complex object, yet each line retains its identity. The coordinates of straight-line endpoints can be used to determine the midpoints for rotation in non-polygonal tessellations. Very detailed figures can easily be created with draw programs.

Requirements for Producing Non-Polygonal Tessellations

A minimum basic set of editing tools and operations is required to produce non-polygonal tessellations.

- A block selection tool, or marquee, to be used with copy or move operations is required. This tool selects all or part of an image by defining a rectangle that encloses the desired part.
- A lasso selection tool is critical, allowing selection of irregular lines or shapes that could not be selected properly with the block selection tool. It will be used to build up tessellating shapes and to select complete shapes for the tessellation operation.
- A move operation is required to perform translations. Moves must be possible in any direction.
- Copy and paste operations are required to tessellate.
- Mirror reflections are required, usually called *horizontal flips* and *vertical flips*.
- Rotation in either direction is desirable and allows more types of tessellations. Many graphic programs limit rotation to 90 degree increments. Rotation in 90 degree increments will generally limit tessellating regions to those based on quadrilaterals.

Techniques for Creating Images

Freehand drawing is the simplest and most direct method of creating graphic images. There is no reason why an image cannot be drawn directly in the graphic program, although some tessellations require precision that might not be achievable by hand.

If a tessellating shape has been created on tissue, thin paper, or clear acetate, it could be taped onto the monitor and traced with the mouse.

However, the technique is prone to parallax error due to the thickness of the monitor's screen. To avoid parallax distortion, do not change your head position once you've started to trace.

Using a Draw Program

A tessellation with a shape based on a rectangle will be constructed here using basic draw functions. We assume the draw program's snap mode is on. In snap mode, ends of lines "snap" to a grid coordinate. The grid display is also on, indicated by the dots on the screen at one-eighth-inch intervals.

With the mouse, click on the empty rectangle tool. Starting in the upper left-hand corner, about one inch from the borders of the drawing area, hold down the mouse button and drag until the rectangle that appears is about one and a half inches wide and one inch deep. Release the mouse button.

Click on the polyline (connected line segment) tool, which will produce an irregular line composed of connected straight line segments. (Some programs have a tool for drawing smooth freehand curves also.) If you are uncertain about which tool to use, click on the Draw menu or look in your software manual.

Starting at the top right-hand corner of the parent rectangle, drag diagonally one third of the way down the side of the parent rectangle. As the line develops, observe it snapping to the grid. Release the mouse button. Now, click on the bottom right-hand corner of the parent rectangle. A line should snap to the vertex of the parent rectangle. The results are illustrated in Figure 3.

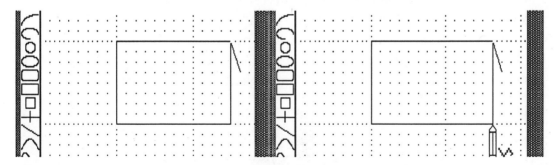

Figure 3. The parent rectangle.

Release the polyline tool by selecting another tool or a menu item. Select the polyline tool again, and draw a multi-segment line similar to that in Figure 4.

The line segments are one to three "snap units" long. The completed line should end at the top left-hand corner of the parent rectangle, forming a modified side.

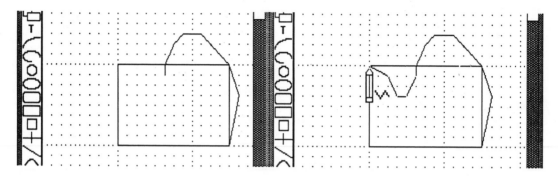

Figure 4. Modified sides of the parent rectangle.

Click on the block select tool. If you are uncertain about which tool to use, click on the Edit menu or look in your software manual. Starting above and to the left of the upper modified side, drag across the modified side until the selection rectangle encloses it. Release the mouse button. The modified side should be surrounded by small squares called hooks. These hooks are used to expand the size of the selected shape. **Do not place the mouse cursor on one of these hooks and drag,** or the altered size will make your project useless. Differently sized shapes will not usually tessellate.

Note that the parent rectangle and a modified side are distinct objects. When the selection rectangle encloses a modified side, part of the parent rectangle is outside the enclosure. Since the parent rectangle is not completely enclosed, it remains unselected. This is one of the most important differences between draw and paint programs.

Choose Copy from the Edit menu, then choose Paste. A paste cursor or even a copy of the original modified side may appear on the screen. If only the cursor appears, click the mouse button. The pasted copy should have selection hooks. Starting from inside the rectangle defined by the hooks of the selected pasted copy, drag it below the parent rectangle. Release the mouse button.

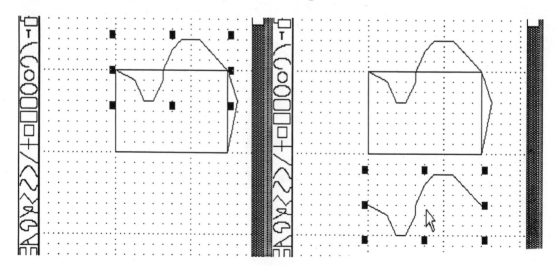

Figure 5. Modified parent rectangle side copied and pasted.

Choose Horizontal Flip from the menu on your system that contains it (usually, Edit, Pick, or Change). With the copied, flipped, modified side still block selected, start from inside the selection block and drag until the side snaps along the bottom of the parent rectangle as in Figure 6.

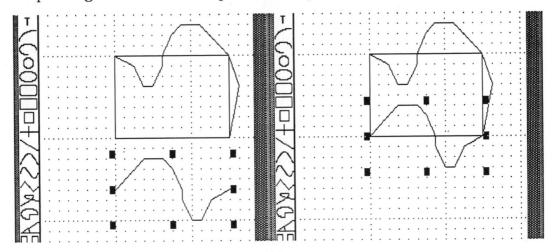

Figure 6. Completed glide reflection of the flipped modified side.

Now, copy, paste, and translate the modified side on the side of the parent rectangle. Note that no horizontal flip is required. Choose the select arrow from either the icon menu or the menu bar. Click on a side of the parent rectangle, and the selection hooks should appear on the parent rectangle as illustrated in Figure 7 (you may have to click several times). Choose Cut from the Edit menu.

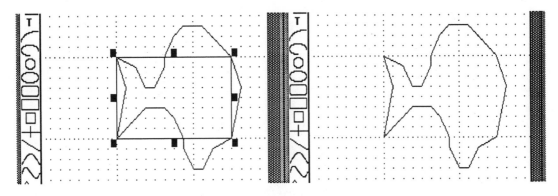

Figure 7. Removal of the parent rectangle.

Tessellating the Sunfish

Block select the tessellating shape. Copy, paste, and then drag the pasted copy until it is merged on the right side of the original tessellating shape. Now, block select the tessellating shape of two figures and copy and paste them. While the pasted copy is still selected, perform a horizontal flip and then merge it onto the bottom of the original pair. You may want to zoom in for more accurate control. As long as some of the selection hooks are visible, you should be able to drag the copy and merge it with the original.

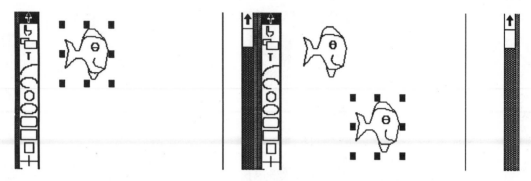

Figure 8. Tessellating shape copied and pasted.

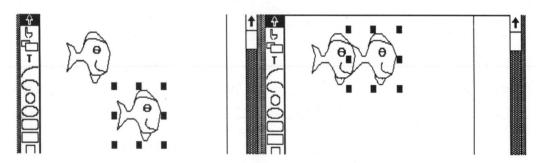

Figure 9. First tessellation completed.

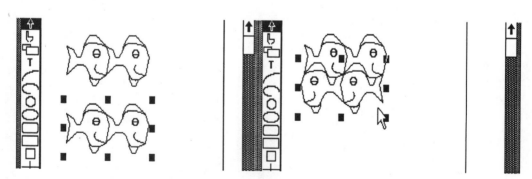

Figure 10. The pair copied and pasted (left), and flipped and merged (right).

Using block select, copy, and paste, you can expand your tessellation.

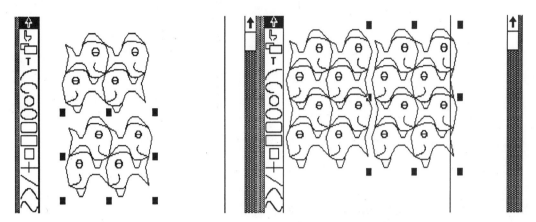

Figure 11. Tessellating with a quartet and octet.

Using a Paint Program

In this section, we will create a simple tessellating shape with freehand drawn lines and the residual corners of a rectangle. The corners will help the alignment while tessellating.

Click on the paintbrush tool to select it. Click on the empty rectangle drawing tool. You may want to select a heavier line weight from a line size dialog box.

A rectangle occupying about one-fourth of the width in the upper third of the paint area will be drawn first. (Don't be misled by the side by side illustrations; they show only half of a screen.) Starting in the upper left-hand corner, about three-fourths of an inch from the border of the paint area, drag until the rectangle that appears is about two inches wide and one and one-half inches deep.

Click on the erase tool. Erase the sides of the rectangle, leaving only a small "leg" on each corner.

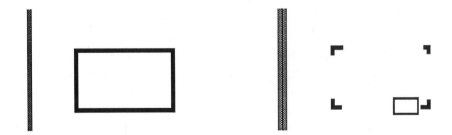

Figure 12. Erasing the rectangle's sides.

Click on the paintbrush tool and draw, freehand, a curve that joins the two top corners.

Figure 13. Random curve joining top corners.

Click on the block select tool. If you are uncertain about which tool to use, click on the Edit menu or look in your software manual. Draw a selection rectangle that includes the curved line and both corners. Choose Copy from the Edit menu, then choose Paste from the Edit menu. Starting from inside the pasted copy, drag the copy below the bottom corners of the residual rectangle. Make sure there is enough space to pass a cursor between the copy and the bottom corners of the residual rectangle.

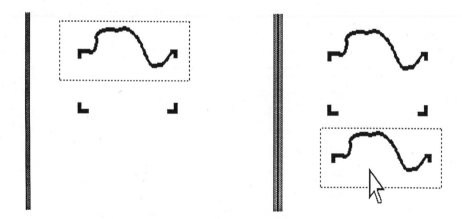

Figure 14. Curved line copied and pasted.

We will now join the corners of the pasted copy and the bottom corners of the residual rectangle. Click on the lasso tool. Again, if you are uncertain about which tool to use, click on the Edit menu or look in your software manual. Trace a freehand line around the pasted copy, and close the loop. (Some paint programs have a selection similar to the block selection tool for this function.)

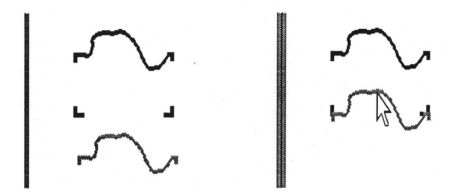

Figure 15. Combining lassoed curve with residual corners.

Starting from over the selected line or from inside the selection box, drag the selected line carefully upwards until the horizontal corner legs coincide and the vertical corner legs align. Release the mouse button.

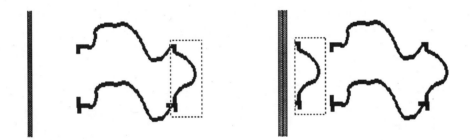

Figure 16. Side curve copied and pasted.

Repeat the procedure for the sides of the rectangle. Draw, copy, paste, lasso, and merge the side curve. You should now have a tessellating shape.

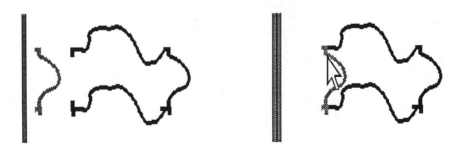

Figure 17. Combining lassoed side curve with residual side corners.

Tessellating the Shape

To tessellate the shape, click on the block selection tool. Draw a selection rectangle to enclose the complete tessellating shape. Choose Copy from the Edit menu, then choose Paste from the Edit menu. Drag the copy to the right of the original, leaving some space between them.

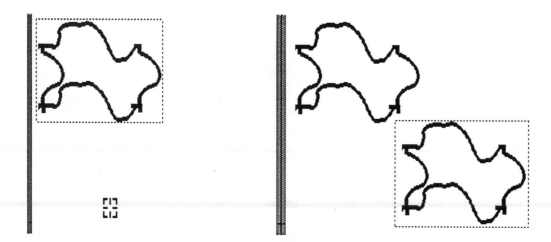

Figure 18. Shape copied and pasted.

Click on the lasso tool. Lasso the complete tessellating shape on the right-hand side. Starting from inside the selected shape, drag carefully toward the original shape until the vertical legs of the corners coincide and the horizontal legs align.

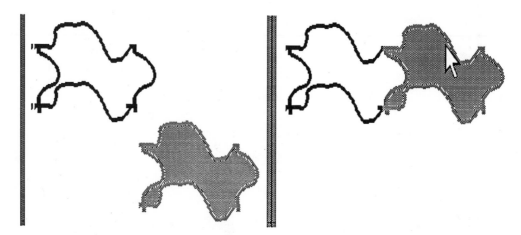

Figure 19. Combining the lassoed shape with the original.

Copy and paste the tessellated pair. Lasso the copy and merge it carefully below the original pair.

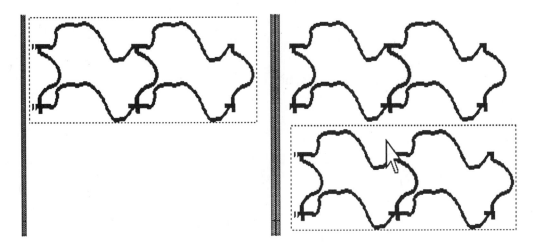

Figure 20. Pair copied and pasted.

You can now tessellate the quartet by using copy and paste followed by a lasso and merge operation.

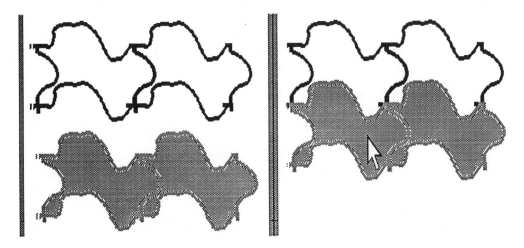

Figure 21. Lassoed copy merged with the original pair.

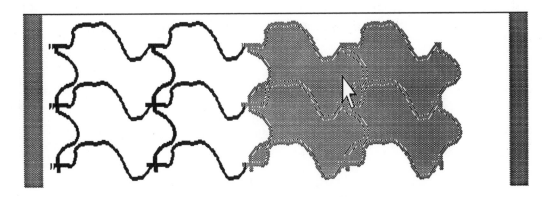

Figure 22. Lassoed and merged quartet.

A Method for More Complex Shapes in Paint Programs

The freehand and tracing methods can be used to create a graphic image in paint programs. Most paint programs have a drawing grid to snap to. The corners of the parent polygon may not be part of the tessellating shape, or the lines may have details too complicated to draw accurately. Mistakes may have to be corrected pixel by pixel. If lines overlap or intersect, you may have to abandon your project.

Another method, using quadruled paper, will generally solve these problems and prove more practical. In this method, a freehand drawing or a tracing with a template on quadruled paper is prepared. Each square represents a pixel. Each square in the quadruled paper that has a line through it is filled in with a pencil. It is preferable to decide which square the line passes through on the paper before you begin plotting in the paint program. The dark squares on the quadruled paper represent pixels that must be turned on.

With the paint program in zoom mode, the pixel elements are turned on as you follow in succession the dark squares on the quadruled paper. It is a tedious process, but simple figures can be done in a matter of minutes.

Pixel-based mapping techniques are time consuming, but are simple, effective, and may be the only way to produce the desired result. The grid at the end of this section is a compromise of visual acuity, image size, and curve smoothness. Exercise care to ensure that extraneous pixels are not introduced or that pixels are not dropped if your eyes begin to play tricks on you.

A Pixel Map Example

In this example, a non-polygonal tessellating shape drawn on a quadruled grid will be transferred to a paint screen. First, the non-polygonal tessellating shape (in this case, a kite-shaped quadrilateral) and its underlying parent polygon are drawn on grid paper (found at the end of this section).

The shape measures about five inches wide by four inches deep, which allows sufficient working space and gives a reasonable printout (the printed size will vary among paint programs). Note that the parent polygon's corners are inside the squares, rather than at the intersection of the grid lines.

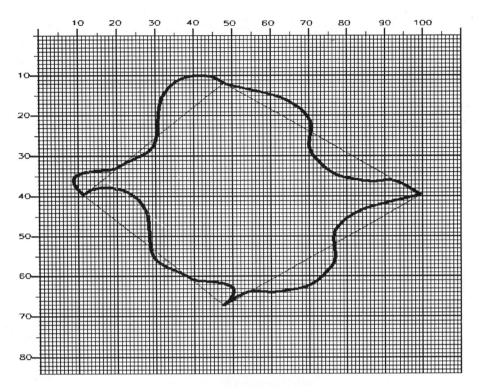

Figure 23. Non-polygonal tessellating shape.

After the shape is drawn, squares of the grid with lines drawn through them are filled in with a pencil—for just one of each pair of modified sides of the parent polygon. The transformed partner of each modified side will be drawn by translation, using the paint, move, and flip operations. Figure 24 shows the completed pixel map.

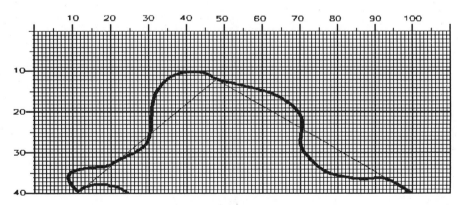

Figure 24. Pencil-filled squares over the parent polygon.

If you have prepared a tessellating template or a rubber stamp as described earlier in this book, you can use either as part of a project in pixel mapping. With the template, draw tightly around the border of the shape on the grid paper with a sharp pencil. With the stamp, print the tessellating shape on the grid paper. In either case, make sure each corner of the parent polygon begins inside a square of the grid. As described previously, fill in the square for just one of each pair of modified sides.

The next step is to convert the squares in the grid paper into pixels in the paint program. Click on the pencil tool, and set the screen to the zoom mode. Starting from halfway down and about three-fourths of an inch from the left side of the screen, plot each filled-in square in succession. In the kite-shaped quadrilateral, the starting point is the square on the horizontal line at the left. Turn on the pixel. Move up one position, and turn on the pixel. Move up and left one position, and again turn on the pixel. Continue plotting until this modified side of the kite-shaped quadrilateral is complete.

The other modified side of the quadrilateral is plotted in the same manner, except for the starting position. A space at the vertex of the two sides is needed to be able to select, with the lasso tool, each modified side independently. Start the second side about twenty pixels to the right of the first. When the plotting is complete, zoom out. The paint screen should look similar to the Figure 25.

Assembling the Shape

The shape is assembled from the two curves just plotted. If the curves are not near the center of the screen, block select and move them there.

Each curve must be duplicated. Block select the left curve, then copy and paste it below and to the left of the original. While it is still selected, choose Horizontal Flip from the menu on your system that contains it (usually, Edit, Pick, or Change). You should see the selected curve change to its mirror image.

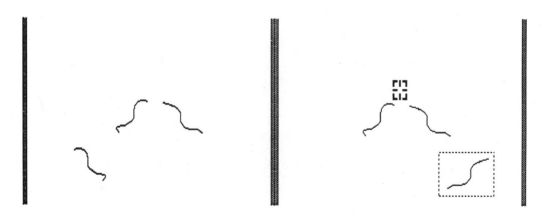

Figure 25. Copied and flipped curves.

Now copy and paste the right curve below and to the right of the original. Flip it as described above. At this point, you may want to save your work.

The next step requires some practice and may not work the first time. The four curves will be joined together using the lasso tool. Click on the lasso tool.

Draw a freehand line to enclose the upper left-hand curve. Starting from inside the selection box or over the selected curve, drag the curve carefully to the right until the two upper curves meet. If they intersect and you have released the mouse button, you may be able to grab the curve again and reposition it.

An error of one pixel can be tolerated, but your tessellation may have bolder curves as a result. If the curves intersect with a four- or five-pixel projection, you will probably have to start over from the point at which you saved your work.

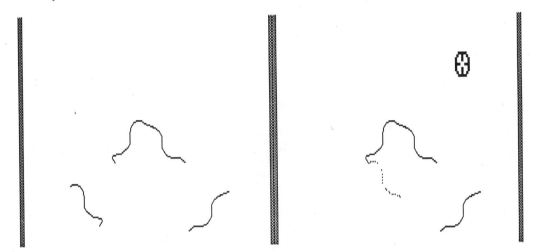

Figure 26. Assembling the tessellating shape.

Now there are three curves to be merged. The curve in the lower left-hand corner of the screen is joined with the upper curve, and the curve in the lower right-hand corner is joined to the other curve. The accuracy should be the same as described above, and can be accomplished within one pixel with practice. After successfully assembling the figure, save your work.

Tessellating with the Shape

Define a block encompassing the assembled tessellating shape. Move the block to the top left-hand corner of the screen. Copy and paste the shape, and move the selected copy to the extreme right-hand side.

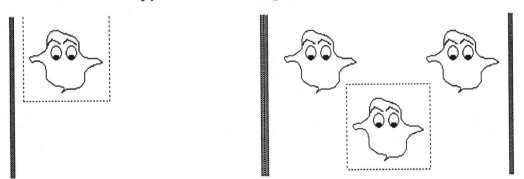

Figure 27. Copied and pasted shapes.

Now, the fun begins. Repeat the paste operation. Voila! Three shapes are on the screen. Let's fill the middle one with paint. Select a color or pattern from the Pallet menu or from the color pallet tool. Now, click on the roller or beaker tool. Place the paint from the beaker or roller inside the middle shape and click.

Figure 28. Selecting a pattern and filling the shape.

If the screen fills completely, the tessellating shape is not a closed figure and must be edited. Don't panic! Choose Undo from the Edit menu. Choose Zoom from the menu on your system that contains it (usually, Pick, Option, Misc, or View). Place or draw the zoomed rectangle over one of the corners where the curves were joined. A small screen will show you the view of the curve you are editing in pixel mode. Fill in the missing pixels by clicking on them. Otherwise, zoom in on the other corners until you find the gap. When you are finished, try the fill operation again. The Undo command will be your greatest friend until fill works properly.

If you want to alternate a solid and an empty shape, you will need to copy and paste a second solid shape. Fill will help to conceal any imperfections when you tessellate.

Figure 29. Copied and pasted solid shape.

Block select the solid shape, flip it horizontally, and select the flipped shape with the lasso tool. Movie it to the left and below the left-hand shape.

Figure 30. First solid shape merged.

Block select, flip, and then move the second solid shape adjacent to the upper figure in the pair.

Figure 31. Second solid shape flipped (left) and second solid shape merged (right).

Lasso the remaining empty figure and move it between the solid figures. Block select, copy, and paste the quartet. Move the copy until it is clear of the original quartet. Lasso the copy and merge the two quartets, overlapping one of the figures in the shape.

Figure 32. Quartet shape merged with overlap.

Repeat until you have tessellated the entire paint canvas.

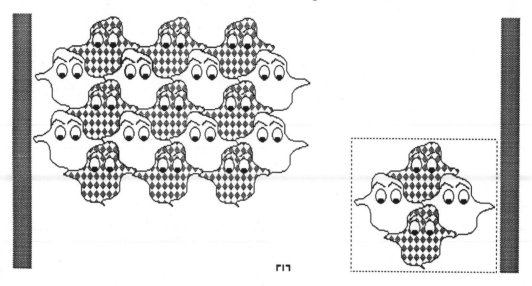

Figure 33. Tessellation with pasted copy ready for tessellating.

Using a Scanner

A classroom full of students who have too many or too few pixels after plotting their figures is a prescription for bedlam. One way to avoid this is to use a hand scanner. An inexpensive hand scanner will centralize the conversion from paper drawing to a paint image and save time.

Only one scanner is required in a classroom, as it takes less than a minute or so to convert a student's tessellating shape into a paint image. The student scans the shape, saves the scanned image on a disk, loads it into a computer, and tessellates the shape immediately in a paint program.

The hand scanner may use an abbreviated paint program not suitable for a complete tessellation project. It would be wise to confirm that the picture storage format of the scanned image is compatible with the paint program being used.

Grid

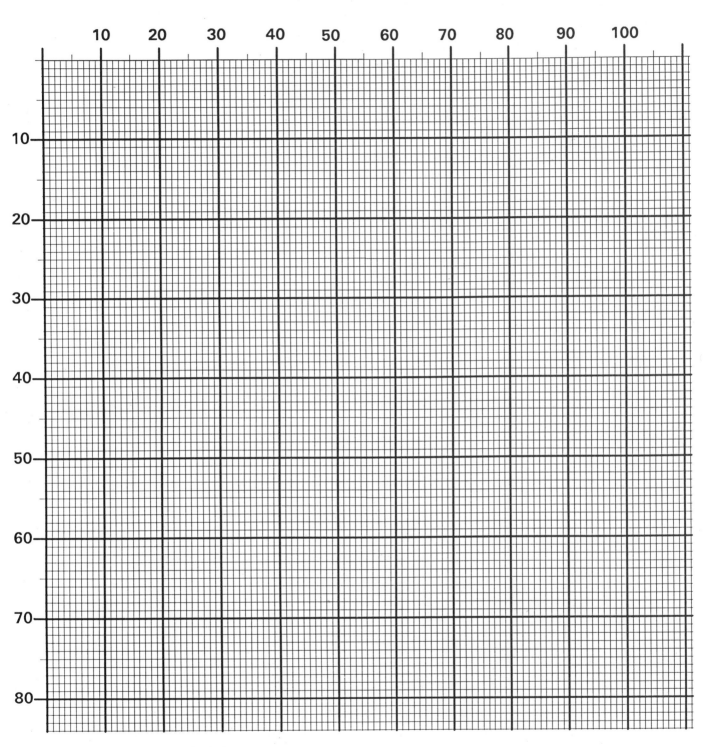

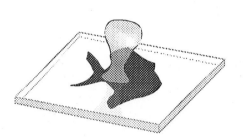
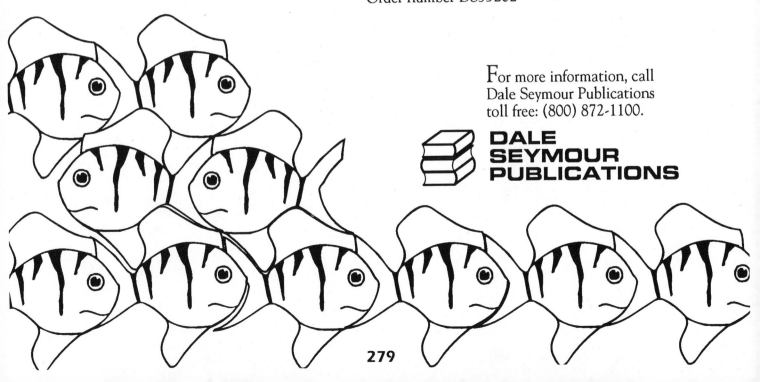

Filling a plane with a pattern, without gaps and without overlaps . . .

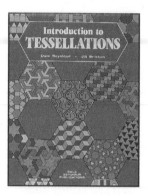

Introduction to Tessellations
by **Dale Seymour and Jill Britton**
264 pages

A clear, understandable introduction to tessellations and other intriguing geometric designs. Written for teachers of grades 6–12, this complete resource contains hundreds of fascinating examples that explore:
- polygons
- regular polygons and combinations of regular polygons
- Escher's tessellations
- Islamic art designs
- tessellating letters
    . . . and much more
Order number DS07901

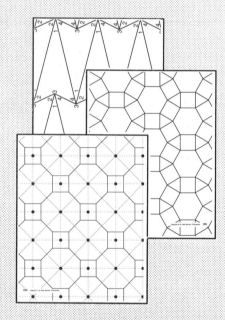

Tessellation Teaching Masters
by **Dale Seymour**
288 pages

This companion book to *Introduction to Tessellations* contains more than 270 full-page tessellating design patterns. Reproduce them to give students practice creating their own patterns or to use as overhead transparencies.
Order number DS07900

Tessellation Winners: original student art
104 pages

The results of a contest in which students submitted original, black-and-white tessellating designs. You and your students will be fascinated by the variety of designs and subjects—and may be inspired to create your own! Includes an introduction to tessellations and a description of the contest.

Order number TS21108

Students and Teachers:

Enter Our Third

TESSELLATION ART CONTEST

Win Dale Seymour Publications Merchandise

See Your Tessellation in Print!

Winners will receive a copy of a book featuring the winning designs, as well as a copy of *Introduction to Tessellations* by Dale Seymour and Jill Britton. The top winners will also receive a $50 gift certificate for merchandise carried by Dale Seymour Publications.

Contest Rules on Reverse

Contest Rules

1. Each entry must be submitted on two sheets of unlined 8½-by-11-inch white paper.

2. On the first sheet, draw the generating polygon with modifying curves superimposed in their appropriate locations. Modifying curves may be transformed by any of these procedures: translation, rotation, reflection, and glide reflection. The resulting shape should not exceed 3 inches in diameter in any direction. Do not show added details on this first sheet.

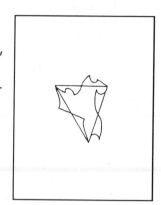

3. On the second sheet, show the completed tessellation with interior details added. Make all markings with black ink, lead pencil, or a computer printer. Do not use color or pencil shading.

4. All drawings must be the original work of a teacher or of a student enrolled in one of the grades K–12 or college on the submission date.

5. Computer-generated entries will be judged separately from hand-drawn designs.

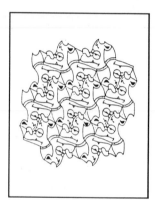

6. Mail entries, **along with a completed entry form,** by June 30, 1994, to TESSELLATION ART CONTEST, Dale Seymour Publications, P.O. Box 10888, Palo Alto, CA 94303. Keep a copy of the submitted artwork.

7. By submitting your artwork, you agree that all rights in that artwork, including all copyrights, are assigned to and become the property of Dale Seymour Publications, and shall be considered "work made for hire" under the copyright act. Entries cannot be returned.

8. For a list of winners, send a self-addressed stamped envelope, Attention: Tessellation Contest Winners, after October 1, 1994.

Entry Form

Name _____

Grade_____ (the grade you are now in or have most recently completed)

School_____ Teacher_____

School Address _____

Home Address _____

I verify that this is my original artwork, and I understand that it will become the property of Dale Seymour Publications as a "work made for hire" under the copyright act.

Signature_____

Parent's Signature _____
    (student and parent or guardian must both sign for students under 18 years of age)

For teachers of students submitting artwork: I give permission for my name to accompany this student's artwork if it appears in forthcoming Dale Seymour Publications material.

Teacher's Signature _____